# Abou

Before becoming a professional entertainer in 1988, Jim Haynes taught in schools and universities from outback New South Wales to Britain and back again. He has two master's degrees in Literature from New England University and the University of Wales.

Jim won the Bush Laureate Book of the Year award in 1996 for his collection of verse, *I'll Have Chips*, and again in 2001 for his compilation, *An Australian Heritage of Verse*. He is the author of a volume of stories, *Memories of Weelabarabak — Stories of a Bush Town*, and the very successful *Great Australian Book of Limericks* and *An Australian Treasury of Popular Verse*.

Jim has released many albums of his own songs, verse and humour and has won the Comedy Song Of The Year award four times at the Tamworth Festival (including the hits, *Don't Call Wagga Wagga Wagga* and *Since Cheryl Went Feral*).

# GREAT
## AUSTRALIAN
## DRINKING
## STORIES

# GREAT
# AUSTRALIAN
# DRINKING
# STORIES

## JIM HAYNES

ABC
Books

Published by ABC Books for the
AUSTRALIAN BROADCASTING CORPORATION
GPO Box 9994 Sydney NSW 2001

First published September 2003

ISBN 0 7333 1326 4.

Set in 11pt Berkeley Book
Colour reproduction by Colorwize
Design by Fisheye Design
Cover photography: Adrian Dreyer
Printed in Australia by Griffin Press, Adelaide

*This one's for Russell Hannah ...*
*Here's cheers Big Russ ...*

## Thanks

Russell Hannah for the suggestions.
Jacqueline Kent for the advice and quality control.
Stuart Neal for the idea and the support.
Stephen Abbott for persevering.
Sally Cohen for the typing.
Robyn for everything else.

# Contents

## The Enlightenment

## The Reformation

# Drinking in Australia
## A Sketchy History

The Australian character seems to be inextricably linked to alcohol. "Easy-going", "tolerant" and "fond-of-a-drink" are qualities, indeed clichés, that occur again and again when Australian stereotypes are being portrayed both at home and overseas.

Did this develop as a result of the pioneer, rough-and-ready nature of our first hundred years of European settlement? Was it allied to the large percentage of Irish and Cockney migrants, who already had a "drinking culture", in those early years? Or was it more to do with the male-dominated nature of Australian frontier society in the nineteenth century?

Of course it is possible to argue quite simplistically that, with a population consisting entirely of convicts, soldiers, sailors and children born out of wedlock in prison hulks, the First Fleet set a national trend for drunkenness and tolerance that could never be entirely reversed. It should be realised that the British discovered and settled this continent at a time when there was an extraordinarily widespread acceptance of alcohol throughout British society, but especially in the navy. You have only to read accounts of British naval and merchant voyages in the eighteenth and nineteenth centuries to understand the huge role played by "grog" — chiefly rum, brandy for officers — in the daily life of a British vessel.

Reading accounts of Cook's voyages gives a special insight. Considered a very firm and fair commander, Cook encouraged the making and consumption of fruit-based home brew (a "jungle-juice" that might or might not have helped ward off scurvy) and his crew were very often more drunk that sober. The German botanist Johann Forster, who went on Cook's second voyage, described the crew as "solicitous to get very drunk, though they are commonly solicitous about nothing else".

Of course, alcohol and drunkenness have been around almost as long as human beings. Appreciation of alcohol is one blessing, among many, passed down to other Western civilisations by the ancient Greeks. The American writer and observer of human behaviour Ambrose Bierce (1842–1914) described Bacchus as "a convenient deity invented by the ancients as an excuse for getting drunk". But he also noted that alcohol was not a feature of all cultures: "When pitted against the hard-drinking Christians the abstemious Mohametans go down like grass before the scythe."

And his comment on British colonisation was: "In India one hundred thousand beef-eating and brandy-and-soda guzzling Britons hold in subjection two hundred and fifty million vegetarian abstainers of the same Aryan race." Bierce, of course, was a well-known cynic.

Nevertheless, it was this British society, largely accepting of alcoholic excess, that established colonies in Australia between 1788 and 1836 and it was the British Navy and merchant fleet, with their easy acceptance of drunkenness as part of everyday life, that provided the only real link between Europe and those colonies.

Although our national day is 26 January, the day the ships of the First Fleet moved from Botany Bay to Port Jackson, the male convicts were disembarked and the British flag was raised, perhaps we should spare a thought for 6 February. On the evening of that day, following the disembarkation of the female convicts and extra rations of rum all round, there developed, in the words of historian Manning Clark, "a drunken spree that ended only when the revellers were drenched by a violent rainstorm".

Early in 1793, just after Arthur Phillip had returned to Britain and left Major Francis Grose temporarily in charge of the fledgling colony, an American ship with the ironic name of the *Hope* sailed into Sydney with a cargo that included 7500 gallons of rum. The captain, one Benjamin Page, refused to sell his cargo except in one lot, including the rum.

The colony had almost starved three years earlier and all supplies were scarce. In light of this and partly to prevent the captain from charging extortionate prices and holding the colony to ransom, the officers of the NSW Corps banded together with Grose's blessing to purchase the entire cargo. This gave them a monopoly on rum, which they exploited whenever a new ship arrived in the colony.

Until 1814 rum became the accepted currency in New South Wales. Soldiers were paid in rum, as were convicts who worked on officers' land. According to historian George Mackaness, in 1806 "The population of Sydney … was divided into two classes, those who sold rum and those who drank it."

This monopoly by the officers of what became known as the Rum Corps led eventually to the corruption that caused the so-called Rum Rebellion of 1808, when the Corps successfully rose up against the governor of the day, William Bligh.

In order to maintain a more usual style of authority, Bligh's successor Lachlan Macquarie arrived with his own regiment in 1810 and the Rum Corps was disbanded. A canny Scot, Macquarie cleverly established a currency by purchasing a cargo of 10,000 Spanish dollars in 1814 and having the centre cut out of every coin. This had the double purpose of providing two coins of different denominations and rendering the coins useless outside the colony, so the currency remained in New South Wales. This strange coin, known as the "holey dollar" (the bit in the middle, of much less value, was known as the "dump") replaced rum as the official currency after twenty-three years.

Macquarie was to write another chapter in the alcoholic history of New South Wales. In order to further control the rum trade he gave the monopoly to import the spirit to a group of businessmen. In exchange they built Sydney's first hospital, which still exists. So, Sydney's first major public institution was built in exchange for rum, and was known for years as the Rum Hospital.

There is, of course, no alcoholic history of Australia before 1788 as Aboriginal society had remained grog-free for 60,000 years. The devastating impact of the British invasion on Aboriginal society has been well documented. The clash of two cultures, one with a long social history of drinking and with no such background, could have only one sad result.

The extreme impact of alcohol on Aboriginal life and culture was noted and lamented within the first years of settlement. Many settlers, as Manning Clark records, were "… appalled by the disastrous effects of civilization on the natives, many of whom became hopeless drunkards, prepared to fight, dance, indeed do anything for the temporary gratification to be obtained from a bottle of rum". Sadly alcohol, one of the most devious weapons of the invader, has continued to provide special problems for the Aboriginal population for over two hundred years.

Even though things were not much better back home in Britain, Australia's drinking reputation was well established by 1840, when Archdeacon Jeffrey noted that "England is becoming the greatest drunkard in the world, except her progeny New South Wales who is said, if it is possible, to drink even deeper still."

In the first sixty years of European settlement, Australia's population spread well ahead of any authority. Various governors attempted to control this expansion into land which wasn't surveyed or owned by the Crown, but it was a losing battle, as was any attempt to regulate or control the production and selling of alcohol in these areas. So the shanty or sly grog shop became the standard drinking establishment of the colony. The quality of the grog offered was dreadful, sometimes fatal, but the climate was hot, men worked at hard physical work and women were scarce (indeed, for much of the nineteenth century men outnumbered women by four to one).

Although Australians were to become known as great beer drinkers, beer was not the main alcoholic choice until late in the century; ale was merely one form of "grog". In 1860 a rather frustrated temperance crusader, Nathaniel Pidgeon, noted that, "By a rough calculation, it would appear that one gallon of beer, 1 1/2 pints of brandy, 1 1/4 pints of gin, and a quart of rum has arrived for every man, woman and child in the colony! It is surely high time for the friends of humanity to bestir themselves!"

Friends of humanity, however, were not particularly thick upon the ground in most areas of the continent at the time. Indeed, thanks partly to the gold rushes, the kind of friendship that was developing was known as "mateship", and part of mateship was a very strong dependence on drinking as a bonding and social experience among men.

This anonymous rhyme sums up Australian drinking habits of the time:

*Now Louis likes his native wine and Otto likes his beer,*
*The Pommy goes for "half and half" because it gives him cheer.*
*Angus likes his whisky neat and Paddy likes his tot,*
*The Aussie has no drink at all — he likes the bloody lot!*

With widespread refrigeration and ice production in the 1880s and 1890s beer became the standard drink for most Australian men, which is, I suppose, not surprising given the climate and the general outdoor style of work at the time.

While twentieth century Australia remained a basically beer-drinking nation, all the alcoholic trends that developed in other

Western nations were also experienced here. Cocktail drinking became trendy and popular in the 1920s and 1930s and awareness of more sophisticated food and wine consumption developed slowly after World War II. New "boutique" beers and fruit drinks became fads in the 1980s, and their popularity has continued to grow.

Rum remained a popular drink, perhaps partly because of tradition and partly because of the sugar industry that developed in Queensland from the 1860s. Brandy, whisky and gin were also popular, particularly among the middle classes, and there was sherry for the ladies. While toleration of alcoholic excess was the norm among men, it was, after those early riotous years of the colony, rarely extended to women.

Wine was one of the first crops grown in the colony and regions like the Hunter Valley have a long and praiseworthy history of producing great wines from the earliest days of settlement. In South Australia German migrants and other pioneer families had established a tradition of great wine production by the late nineteenth century in areas like Barossa, Clare, McLaren Vale and Langhorne Creek.

But general appreciation of wine did not really come to Australia until the 1980s, when the wine industry really took off. Its spectacular growth coincided with a changing attitude to drinking generally. Australia has slipped well down the table of beer drinkers, for example, from number one in the world for consumption per head of population in the 1950s to a miserable tenth in 1999.

Changes in licensing laws greatly affected drinking habits in Australia. Pubs were forced to close at 6pm during the 1940s and 1950s. The idea was that this would improve family life and encourage temperance. What resulted, of course, was the notorious "six o'clock swill". Early closing simply led to men drinking as much as they could as fast as they could from the time they finished work until six every evening. Even after its demise early closing had established a tradition of a regular "drinking session" in the evenings after work.

Today Australia is a complex society with different drinking cultures. Many changes have occurred in recent times. We tend to drink more often with meals than before or after them, as in the past. We drink more wine and less beer. We are perhaps more temperate due to strict drink-driving laws and a growing awareness of the harmful effects of alcohol on our health and our society. On the other hand, many Australians are drinking at a younger age, and binge drinking and alcohol abuse are more discussed and worried over than ever.

Attitudes to drinking in our society will naturally vary from total acceptance to extreme intolerance. Opinions about Australian drinking have always differed. Visitors to our shores have had mixed reactions to our drinking habits. In 1873 English author Anthony Trollope found our drunkenness to be a reflection of some of our better characteristics: "Australian drunkenness," he said, "so far as it exists, is not of the English type. It is more reckless, more extravagant, more riotous, to the imagination of man infinitely more magnificent; but it is less enduring, and certainly upon the whole less debasing."

A century later, however, in 1975, Danish journalist Poul Nielsen was moved to comment, "I have felt scared since I arrived in Sydney, in fact I feel more relaxed in New York than here. There is something desperate about the way people drink here." If he thought that of Sydney I wonder what he would have made of Darwin.

Perhaps the disparity in opinion here has something to with the nationality of the observer. Or perhaps it has more to do with the company Trollope and Nielsen kept while visiting our shores, or social changes over the intervening century.

Contradictory opinions exist also on the home front. In the year 1974, for instance, an article appeared in the *Australian Church Record* describing the evils of drink inflicted on eleven year olds in state schools: "The girls had their first cooking lesson. The tasty morsel to be cooked was rum balls. Whether rum essence or the real jungle juice scarcely matters. Small girls were to be introduced to this highly desirable alcoholic flavour. Perhaps it is part of the modern approach to cooking, which is to saturate almost everything in some form of alcohol and give it a French name."

In the same year advertising agency executive John Singleton commented quite matter-of-factly that, "The advertising industry lives a very cyclical sort of life. December is the month for getting pissed."

How does the average Australian handle these contradictory views of disapproval and acceptance? How do we cope with attempts to restrict and control our drinking and yet remain true to the Aussie belief in a "fair go"? Perhaps some insight can be gained from this item which appeared a few years ago in the *Sydney Morning Herald*'s Column 8: "By chance a colleague booked into a north Queensland motel before learning that its dining-room was not licensed. 'Think nothing of it,' said the waitress. 'If you want a bottle of beer with your steak just say Steak and Laundry. It doesn't show on the records.'"

Which brings us to the subject of anecdotes, stories, verse and literature about Australian drinking, which brings us to the subject of this book. Here is a collection that I hope is both entertaining and thought-provoking, a collection that I hope will neither drive you to drink nor turn you away from the pleasures of alcohol in moderation. So, please, grab a glass of your favourite beverage and read on.

# The Roaring Days

# Introduction

"Roaring drunk" … it's a common expression and has been throughout Australia's short European history. It is used to indicate that those who are inebriated are having a rollicking good time, their behaviour becoming outrageous, reckless and daring as opposed to introverted, depressive and vindictive.

Rightly or wrongly, this is the type of drunkenness which has been tolerated, forgiven and even rather admired by a large section of Australian society for about two hundred years. It is a type of drunkenness associated with good times, mateship, camaraderie, nostalgia and outrageous, though often amusing, social behaviour.

Of course it is also the type of drunkenness that a sober person finds extremely childish and often boorish. But arriving late at a boozy party is never a good idea if one wants to feel close to and comfortable with one's fellows.

In Australia there is often a real forgiveness of "roaring drunk" behaviour and a feeling of warmth and concern for the drinker. Drunken deeds often become the stuff of local or family legend. There is a real affection for the uncle or mate who is "very funny" or "outrageous" when he's "had a few". The cultural shame associated with social drunkenness that one finds in Asia and many European countries, like Spain and Portugal, is almost nonexistent in Australia.

Why is this? Well, there are many probable reasons for the toleration of this form of drunkenness in Australia.

One could postulate that Australia has fewer social restrictions and patterns built up over generations than other nations, or that Australia was, by its nature as a migrant and convict settlement, bound to develop social traits that opposed authority and conformity.

Conversely, one could argue that the British colonies of Australia, as a result of their "Britishness" and "colonial-ness" quickly developed very restrictive and conservative social attitudes which required some form of social rebellion, and drink was the most available means to this end.

However it developed, Australian society still has a very tolerant attitude towards alcohol and a very real suspicion of intolerant or "wowserish" attitudes to drinking. The need to be a drinker to be fully included in the male-dominated society of working-class Australia was, until recently, a very palpable social force and the Barry Humphries' quote which prefaces the first story of this collection, satirically intended or not, is still a commonly held belief.

So here is a batch of stories which in some way celebrate the social gift of alcohol. Riotous evenings of complete surrender to Bacchus, deals sealed with booze, grave social occasions subverted by drink and Lawson's apology and justification for drunkenness.

Reading these stories one is struck by the obvious familiarity many of the authors have with their subject material. Henry Lawson, Lennie Lower and Kenneth Cook are to be found again and again in this collection. Perhaps it is apt to note here that Lawson and Lower were both alcoholics themselves and their work is infused with a profound sense of the acceptance of alcohol as a essential element of human existence. The brief pieces that represent their work in this section are good examples of their differing attitudes to alcohol.

For Lawson there is a melancholy acceptance of the part played by drink in a drinking man's life, indeed, his letter to the *Bulletin* is a sort of Aussie alcoholic's manifesto.

For Lower the subject of drink provided yet another chance for social satire, playfulness and cynicism. While I have found Lower's attitude to be typical of many intelligent hard drinkers, few of them wrote as well, or as amusingly, as Lennie Lower.

"One Hundred Stubbies" is a fascinating look at that old Aussie obsession with how much a man can drink. This is often taken to be a measure of the man and is a quality admired in some sections of Aussie male society.

Kenneth Cook was a particularly accurate observer of outback life and while his stories included in this book are quite objective accounts of alcohol-related incidents, one can detect also a sense of acceptance of the realities of alcohol and it is no surprise that Cook was a man who "enjoyed a drink", indeed he called himself a "lay alcoholic".

This all seems to point toward the veracity of the old maxim and schoolyard retort, "it takes one to know one". And it certainly seems to ring true also in the case of "A Journalist's Funeral". Although I know nothing at all about its author, an anonymous *Bulletin* writer of the 1890s, his account of the prophetic nightmare of his own funeral seems to display a very real understanding of both the social behaviour of habitual drinkers and the sad realities of the world of journalism. I find this century-old story quite undated and very amusing in its unerringly accurate account of the way members of a traditionally hard-drinking profession react to a colleague's passing when drink is part of the funeral rites.

The Sandman story that begins this collection displays, like all Sandman stories, the objectivity of the social outsider. It is a totally non-judgmental account of another man's alcoholic odyssey. It demonstrates, like the Kenneth Cook story, an acceptance of the Aussie drinking culture along with a certain sense of wonder and admiration for the alcoholic capacity of the protagonist.

The unashamed pleasure of alcoholic indulgence is the subject of quite a few of the pieces in this section. In "The Speech" Lower's readers are made aware of the social efficacy of alcohol and the anti-social horrors of temperance and wowserism by the eloquent Mr Sloove. The fact that he is preaching to the converted, along with the fact that he concludes his sermon by falling off a table, certainly don't lessen the beauty of his logic.

Although most of the characters in Steele Rudd's story, "The Evening Before Leaving Home", are horrified and ashamed of Dad's behaviour it is obvious that Rudd was very aware of the unbridled joys of inebriation. Whether this was from first-hand or second-hand experience I don't know. Rudd had a reputation for being quite a serious-minded fellow but he certainly drank socially and was well acquainted with the life he is portraying here, having grown up on a selection himself.

The social rituals associated with alcohol range from ethnic to gastronomic and from religious to barbaric. We are always being asked to raise our glasses to something. The old pagan use of alcohol as a method of pledging and bonding is alive and well in many societies and has a strong tradition down under, so it is appropriate that Australia's most admired alcoholic, Henry Lawson, gets the final word again.

*The night too quickly passes and we are growing old,*
*So let us raise our glasses and toast the days of gold,*
*When finds of wondrous treasure set all the south ablaze,*
*And you and I were faithful mates, back in the roaring days!*

> "Beware the evils of temperance and sobriety and embrace
> the worship of the bottle!"
>
> DAVID IRELAND, 1971

# The Speech [from *Here's Luck*]
## Lennie Lower

The party had quietened down considerably. There was a strip poker party in the dining room and a drinking party in the bedroom adjoining. Couples whispered here and there in corners, a few stupid ones sang determinedly around the piano and the weaker vessels slept and mumbled in strange attitudes. I strolled past the strip-poker table, noticing as I passed that most of the girls evidently could not play poker and that Smacker was sitting behind a routine flush. I watched him see a bet of one camisole and raise it a pair of suspenders and a singlet, and then joined the other party.

I found myself a couple of bottles of whisky and sat down. "You're not going to drink that on your own?" exclaimed Temple, who was lying on the floor next to me with his head propped up on his elbow.

"There's plenty over there for you," I replied, pointing to the stack.

"But, man, you'll kill yourself!"

"I'm not worrying about that," I said, putting the bottle to my mouth.

"He's drinking it out of the bottle!" he shouted to the company.

"Etiquette, mon!" said McLavish, shaking his finger at me.

"'Member yer etti-hic!"

"Leave 'im alone," growled Woggo, thickly.

"Am I to sit here and watch a man drink himself to death!" shouted Temple. "I say nothing against a man drinking, but to drink like that … I regard it as my duty and as the duty of all of you, to stop this man, in his own interests."

"Talk sense!"

"I am talking sense. It is for his own good and the good of those associated with him. Mr Sloove," he said, pointing to the politician, "and myself are the only two sober men here!"

"Bung," said Woggo, nudging the heavyweight. "Bowl 'im and stack 'im."

Bung Thomas rose unsteadily to his feet and rolled toward Temple.

"Erpologize, or I'll breathe on yer," he growled.

Temple mumbled a sullen apology and subsided, glaring at me.

"Gentlemen," announced Mr Sloove. "Mr Temple has just mentioned my name to you and accused me of being sober. I must admit the charge while not agreeing with his opinions of our worthy host."

I bowed as well as I could, lying on the floor.

"As a matter of fact," he continued, "my presence here tonight is mainly due to my young friend from the *Daily Herald*, Mr Wills. Knowing that Mr Gudgeon is a gentleman well liked and respected in the locality, and an old resident of the district, I thought to seize the opportunity to combining business with pleasure by addressing a few remarks —"

"Siddown!"

"I will not weary you with —"

"Chuck 'im out!"

"Briefly, the position —"

Woggo rose to his feet. "Bung," he called.

Mr Sloove sat down.

"Yes, Corpsey? Wot do you want?" said Slatter belligerently as a head poked around the door.

"Sling me a couple them sheets," said Corpsey, nodding toward the bed.

The sheets were passed out and presently he appeared among us wrapped up like a Roman emperor.

"Toughest game I ever played in," he muttered, dragging the rest of the bedclothes off the bed. "If Smacker was playing poker in Klondike 'e'd 'ave been shot as soon as he shuffled."

He threw the bedclothes into the adjoining room.

"Give one of them sheets to the fair-'aired sheila," he cried. "She's got a cold."

Another loser strolled in, barefooted and holding his trousers up, and brought his banjo with him. McLavish sang "Annie Laurie" and cried bitterly. The milkman sang "The Star Spangled Banner", "O Heart Bowed Down", "Paddy McGinty's Goat", finished up with a little yodelling, and then went to sleep. We had "Sweet Adeline" three or four times and we were all feeling pleasantly sad and comradely when Mr Sloove rose for the second time. His face was flushed and he mounted the only chair in the room and stood swaying uncertainly.

"Gentlemen," he said, speaking with painstaking distinctness, "with Mr Gudgeon's permission and in the distinguished presence of Mr Bung Thomas, the greatest heavyweight Tasmania has ever produced, and also that well-known sporting man, Mr Woggo Slatter, I would like to say a few words."

"'Ear! 'Ear!" cried Thomas and Slatter.

"Our respected friend, Mr Temple, who has just been carried outside, saw fit to make a few remarks with which I entirely disagree. It is on the subject of drink and drinkers that I wish to speak."

Mr Sloove seemed to have captured the interest of the assembly.

"Of course," he was saying, "there are people who will never drink. Subnormal freaks, or misguided in their early youth.

"There are others who may be converted," continued Mr Sloove. "I have to my eternal credit one outstanding case. He was a miserable man for whom life held but little interest. Taciturn and morose, he was, wrapped in his petty ideas of life and pleasure. In fact, gentlemen, he had never had a proper drink in his life."

There was a mutter of amazement from the audience. I noticed the young man from the *Daily Herald* taking shorthand notes.

(Our party was described as an orgy and a saturnalia in the next evening's paper. The hound! I got a copy of Mr Sloove's speech from him, though. Best speech I ever heard.)

"I persuaded this man," continued Sloove, "to taste, just taste my fine old brandy, two cases of which comprised my late father's estate. He was run over by a bus and couldn't finish it. He died a broken-hearted man. Sometimes I think he haunts the cellar, spirit calling to spirit, but I digress.

"I offered this poor, water-logged waif the brandy.

"He smelt it. He sipped it. He sipped again, eagerly. He tossed it off. Then turning to me, he clasped my hand, a look of reverent wonder in his eyes. 'To think …' he said, 'all these years. And I never knew. I never knew! … *Fill it up again!*'"

A burst of cheers awoke Simpson, who started to clap.

"Now, any night, I can go to his flat and find him lying under the table, happy."

The speaker waved his hand.

"Alcohol! The last gift of the relenting gods. The simple word that makes life's crossword puzzle easier to elucidate."

"How many paltry figures have ranted against it, shrieked their censure," he cried, "and faded back to the earth from which they come — to fertilise the vines.

"Gaze on your glass of beer."

We gazed.

"See how the lambent, lazy bubbles drift to the top, as men drift through life; linger a while in the froth, and burst of old age, or are cut off in their prime in Fate's thirsty gulp. This scourge, this shame, this liquid degradation, what is it?"

"'Ere!" protested Simpson, angrily.

"It links the extremes of mankind in one common friendly girdle. The labourer disturbing the rocks of ages with his pick, and Shakespeare in his favourite inn, and Attila, the Scourge of God, who died of too much mead."

"What's this mead? Where c'n it be got?"

"Look here, Simpson," I whispered. "Don't interrupt again. This man's a genius. Listen to him."

"Noah," shouted Sloove, "the greatest navigator of all times; cooped in the ark with his relations and a lot of other wild animals, drifting in a landless world. Chosen from countless teetotallers drowned in their favourite drink; he landed at last on the lonely peak of Ararat. When the awful responsibility of beginning a new world had eased, what happened?"

Woggo shook his head vigorously.

"The Bible says that his son found him lying in the vineyard, his back teeth awash and a happy, boozed smile on his face."

McLavish looked up.

"Behold your Robbie Burns. He died. Certainly, who doesn't? He drank himself to death! What of it? For every man who dies of drink, a thousand die of dinner-distended stomachs. Ask the man who owns one."

"What the hell are you looking at me for?" I demanded, as Stanley eyed my vest with a silly grin on his face.

"Says the earnest reformer," continued Sloove, "supposing that, instead of drinking whisky, you drank milk. Look at the benefits to your health, your pocket, and the race in general. Against this horrible suggestion there is, thank heaven, a stonewall fact, a gesture in granite, one great unshakable answer, 'I don't like milk.'

"It is an axiom of economists that supply follows demand like the blood follows a punch on the nose. We want beer. Therefore there is beer. Peer into the murky mystery of your orange phosphate. What do you see? A chemical laboratory. A bit of this being added, a bit of that tipped in. And in the translucent depths of booze? Hop fields, rippling acres of barley, and whistling boys in the sunshine, picking grapes. You would have me drink this coloured eye lotion? Consider, then, this awful possibility.

"Two old friends meet.

"'Bill! Why, you old son of a gun!'

"'Where've you been? Haven't seen you for years!'

"A moment of happy grins, of surging happy memories, of handshakes truly meant.

"'Well, well, well!'

"Glad. Awkward. Lost for words.

"'Come and have an orangeade!'"

He paused, while a wave of horror swept over the company.

"I *ask* you!" he exclaimed passionately.

Sloove cleared his throat.

"Alcohol is a necessity," he said. "The craving for food is recognised as legitimate, even though the rabid vegetarian seeks to snatch the chop from his brother's mouth. Yet I am asked to satisfy my desire for a drink with water! Water! Empty jam tins are all right for goats, but a hungry dog wants meat. We are but dust, add water and we are mud.

"Why, when the world was first made it was all water, until the mistake was seen and rectified, and land made available for hop growing."

"A course," agreed Simpson.

"I don't want to disparage water. It is an excellent medium for sailing boats in, washing, cooking, and irrigation. It is an ingredient of most liquors. But to drink it in its raw state! Watch a drinking fountain in Pitt Street. You'll stand for hours and see it undisturbed, save for the mooning messenger boy who stamps on the button to see the water squirt.

"As to those who have tasted liquor and liked it not, well, they do exist; but about them we need not bother. They are akin to the horse that drinks water and the calf that guzzles milk. Evolution will weed them out. Lack of the booze taste is lack of virility and they cannot survive. Is there any more expressive word in our language than 'Milksop'? And what is it but a weak sopper of milk, a lemonade lapper, a cocoa gargler?

"'Yo! Ho! And a bottle of raspberry!' Absurd, isn't it?"

"My oath, it is."

"Despite our modern education there are fools who have never tasted drink, lunatics who have, and don't like it, and plague spots, positive menaces, who seek to abolish it!"

There was a general movement of uneasiness.

"Ah, friends. If you would learn, come with me beneath the bough. I'll bring the bread and the thou. I can't bear all the expense. We shall transform that wilderness and people it with pink lizards and blue monkeys with hats on. Be saved while the thirst is still on you and you shall have access to a land where every prospect pleases, and only closing time is vile.

"And I, when I have sunk my last pot, when my foot no more rests on the rail, and old Time calls, 'Six o'clock, sir!' then carry me to the strains of the Little Brown Jug and lay me on my bier ... 'And in a winding-sheet of vine-leaf wrapt, so bury me by some sweet garden-side.'

"Till then ... Here's luck!"

There was a moment's silence, then suddenly the assembly burst into a roar of delighted applause. They stamped their feet, whistled piercingly, and cheered and clapped.

Mr Sloove smiled, and attempting a bow, fell off the chair. There were a dozen hands to help him rise.

> **"Never trust a man who doesn't drink."**
>
> BARRY HUMPHRIES, 1965

# My First Literary Lunch
## The Sandman

The following alcoholic adventure coincided with my first ever book deal. I won't mention the publisher, or the person's name, but let's say he's a commissioning editor well-known for his liquid exploits. For convenience sake, I'll call him Stan.

I, that is Sandman, Sandy, or me, am invited to lunch by Stan to discuss the possibility of signing a book deal with his company.

It's a tradition in literary circles that before being signed you're wined and dined. So it's arranged that I meet Stan at the Watson's Bay pub at twelve noon to discuss the deal over lunch.

I'm fifteen minutes late, I'm only a minor celebrity, I can't keep people waiting much longer than that without causing offence.

Stan, in his forties, salt and pepper hair, medium build housed in a laconic demeanour, is sitting at an outside table with a Crown lager standing guard in front of him like a taciturn grenadier. As I join him he suggests a quick beer while we order some wine and, even though the taste of toothpaste is still dominating my mouth, I accept his kind offer. Stan, very near the end of his first beer, orders another one so I'm not left drinking alone. He also orders wine to go with the meal.

It's unseasonably warm and the combination of beer and wine in the afternoon sun soon takes its toll. At the conclusion of our first bottle of wine I'm full of confidence. I tell Stan I can deliver three novellas in two years, no trouble. I'm having difficulty attaching the gs to my -ing words, but I seem to know what I'll be doing in two years' time.

Stan is one beer in front of me and shows no sign of slurring. He's like a cricketer who bowls perfect slower balls with no change in action. As Stan becomes more intoxicated, he appears to be stone cold sober.

The main meal finishes but there are sweets and a second bottle of wine to negotiate. By now it's pushing 2.30pm and we're directly in the sun. As those who have dined at Watson's Bay Hotel will be aware, the afternoon sun shines directly on the outdoor eating area.

The effect of summer sunshine on drinkers is well documented. Apparently it's the same as having three quick schooners on top of what you've already had, spinning around after you scull home brew or drinking wine from a wine bag: you get drunk much quicker.

When we finish the meal and the second bottle of wine, Stan suggests we retire to the front bar and kick on. By now six glasses of wine, a beer and three hours of sunshine have seen me well and truly over the plimsoll.

During the next two hours I consume five schooners of New and Stan drains six. (Since I'm lagging behind, Stan takes matters into his own hands and orders another beer for himself.) As I watch him I realise that nothing looks more natural than Stan in a public bar studying the racing guide with a beer in front of him and a gasper resting on his lips, like a self-conscious teenager leaning on a wall. I soon realise that if I don't come up with an excuse to escape I'll find myself bum up over the washing basket sometime tonight because it'll be the closest thing I can find when I know I can't make the toilet.

I don't want to appear weak because I know writers are celebrated for holding their grog, so I come up with a good escape; I tell Stan I have an earache. I buy another round so it seems like I'm a good bloke, but I keep referring to my ear to make my excuse appear more legit. So we finish the round and Stan drops me home in a cab. I'm gone, but I'm not wearing the whirlybird shirt, as my aunt Coral often described people who'd drunk too much.

Within half an hour I'm in an alcoholic coma on my two-seater lounge, but while I grapple with broken sleep, Stan's legendary adventures continue.

I meet Stan quite a few times over the next few months and he eventually fills me in on what happened over the rest of that evening. This account is my own understanding of Stan's shared memories.

Stan's next port of call is the home of some Greek friends in Bondi Junction. He stays there until around 9pm drinking beer and retsina. That's four more hours of drinking on top of his six glasses of wine, two Crownies and seven schooners at the Watson's Bay Hotel. Let's say, and I'm being conservative, he has six beers and three glasses of retsina at Bondi Junction. Let's say that puts him at nine glasses of wine and fifteen beers by 9pm.

His next stop is the Tea Gardens Hotel, Bondi Junction. The Tea Gardens is an old-fashioned pub. The public bar has all the earmarks of a bygone era: tiles, polished wood and that sepia light that gives you the feeling a boy with rickets may come through any minute wheeling a barrow full of rabbits.

Stan is a lover of pub culture; in fact, he has written a book on the subject. He is a wonderful listener and has no trouble assimilating with strangers. He attaches himself to a group of drinkers, some of whom he knows by sight. One is a well-known actor, most of the others are his cronies.

Stan is soon fully accepted into the alcoholic circle and, inevitably, someone asks what he does for a living. Stan truthfully, but perhaps foolishly, replies that he's a commissioning editor for a major publishing house.

Suddenly it appears that everybody in the group is working on a book, or has an idea for a book that will sell a million copies.

One chap says he has a great idea for a tennis book. Stan tells the chap, probably more frankly than he would normally do at the office, that tennis books never sell and he'd never be interested in publishing one.

An argument erupts, with the would-be author yelling at Stan that he doesn't know Arthur from Martha and he should piss off. Sensing a disruption in the ranks the well-known actor intervenes. There is a heated exchange, which ends in an undignified scuffle. When a wild punch is thrown and misses Stan by millimetres, causing his fringe to pulsate like the throat of a courting frog, Stan no longer feels welcome. He picks up his opinions and heads off into the night.

The next stop on Stan's alcoholic odyssey is his dad's place at Five Dock. Time, around midnight. Let's say Stan lasted an hour and a half at the Tea Gardens. Let's say Stan had five schooners. Let's say that places him at twenty beers and nine glasses of wine in twelve hours. It seems that Stan's father also likes a drink and, despite being ill, he is happy to keep his son company until they run out of alcohol sometime around 3am.

Let's say between midnight and 3am there's time for five beers and a couple of scotches. Let's also say Stan's probably feeling bloated by this stage because once you've drunk that much beer it's difficult to keep putting liquid in.

Perhaps Stan's stomach is designed like the *Titanic*, with a series of watertight compartments to stop him going down; at 3am, neither man is satisfied their night is over. Father and son decide to go to a nearby hotel and take advantage of its twenty-four-hour licence.

With his dad, who is still dressed in PJs and dressing-gown, Stan makes the one-kilometre journey to the pub where he is still able to remain upright and communicate well enough to order more drinks.

The publican says on their arrival that he doesn't mind Stan's father coming down the pub when he looks so ill because he's a regular, but he asks could he please not come down in his PJs any more because he scares the other drinkers.

Stan and his dad drink until it's getting light and then Stan, devoted publishing man that he is, says that he fully intends to go to work. He's done it before and he can do it again. So Stan and his dad weigh anchor and cast off for the walk home.

Now, when you're really drunk, a one-kilometre walk can feel like a round-the-world voyage. From all reports, the trip home was rough going for Stan and both he and his dad made rather heavy weather of it. Let's say from 3.30am to 5.30am they managed four beers and two scotches, that puts Stan at twenty-three beers, nine wines and four or five scotches.

As father and son tack into the stiff breeze it all becomes too much for Stan's dad; despite Stan holding onto him, dad falls overboard. As Stan attempts to help his father back into the boat, a passing motorist sees a drunk standing over a much older drunk who is dressed in pyjamas, dressing-gown and slippers. It's 5.45am and the passing motorist finds the scene rather disturbing.

The passing motorist pulls over, gets out of his car, grabs Stan, yanks him off his father, shakes him violently and pushes him away, accusing him in no uncertain terms of trying to roll a poor defenceless wino.

Stan's communication skills are by now somewhat impaired and it takes a while for him to convince the Good Samaritan that he is only trying to help his father get home.

True to his word, Stan makes it to work. In fact he's early, so with time up his sleeve and in need of something to offset the sensations in his stomach, he ventures to the canteen for a sausage sandwich. Then, like a wild animal that removes its kill from view, Stan drags his sandwich back to his office.

Now, a sausage sandwich in oily wrapping paper inside a paper bag is like a Rubik's Cube to a drunk man. It's at this point of the story, as Stan struggles with his sandwich and strains to keep his head upright, that a colleague sticks his head through the door of Stan's office and notices Stan floating there like a specimen in formaldehyde.

The colleague says, "Stan … Stan, mate … I think you should go home." And that's exactly what Stan does.

It's easy to see why Stan is so successful. He works such long hours, his staff really care about him and he can take advice.

"Australians are not a nation of snobs like the English, or of extravagent boasters like the Americans ... they are simply a nation of drunkards."

Marcus Clarke, 1869

## Letter to the *Bulletin* re Drinking
### Henry Lawson

Dear *Bulletin*,

I'm awfully surprised to find myself sober. And, being sober, I take up my pen to write a few lines, hoping they will find you as well as I am at present. I want to know a few things. In the first place: Why does a man get drunk? There seems to be no excuse for it. I get drunk because I'm in trouble, and I get drunk because I've got out of it. I get drunk because I am sick, or have corns, or the toothache: and I get drunk because I'm feeling well and grand. I got drunk because I was rejected; and I got awfully drunk the night I was accepted. And, mind you, I don't like to get drunk at all, because I don't enjoy it much, and suffer hell afterwards. I'm always far better and happier when I'm sober, and tea tastes better than beer. But I get drunk. I get drunk when I feel that I want a drink, and I get drunk when I don't. I get drunk because I had a row last night and made a fool of myself and it worries me, and when things are fixed up I get drunk to celebrate it. And, mind you, I've got no craving for drink. I get drunk because I'm frightened about things, and because I don't care a damn. Because I'm hard up and because I'm flush. And, somehow, I seem to have better luck when I'm drunk. I don't think the mystery of drunkenness will ever be explained — until all things are explained, and that will be never. A friend says that we don't drink to feel happier, but to feel less miserable. But I don't feel miserable when I'm straight. Perhaps I'm not perfectly sober just now, after all. I'll go and get a drink, and write again later.

# One Hundred Stubbies
## Kenneth Cook

To understand how this could happen, you have to know something about where it happened — Coober Pedy, an almost impossible town in the arid centre. Coober Pedy is an opal mining town. The name is Aboriginal for "white man in a hole". The "hole" refers to the mines and to the houses, which are caves dug into the sides of low hills. In the summer the temperature averages around 50 degrees Celsius. You spend most of your time underground or in a pub, or you die.

I had driven up from Adelaide in an air-conditioned car and I thought I was going to die.

I saw Coober Pedy in the distance as thousands of tiny round bubbles in the shimmering desert heat haze. Soon these bubbles resolved themselves into the waste piles from the opal mines that stretch endlessly out from the town in all directions.

The whole area looks as though it is infested by the termites that build those huge nests of mud. Many of the mines are deserted and local legend has it that they contain the bones of reckless men who have welshed on gambling debts or tried robbing mines. I never actually heard of a skeleton being found.

The sight of the pub in Coober Pedy automatically brought my car to a halt. I needed cold beer, and lots of it. The heat out there is almost solid and you can feel it dropping on your head when you step out of the car. I trotted across to the pub, my whole being yearning for beer, totally unaware that I was about to witness an event that would put me off beer drinking for months.

The pub was moderately full of pink men. Almost all the men in Coober Pedy are pink because they are opal miners and the pink dust of the mines becomes ingrained in their skins. Or perhaps they never wash, because the water there is pretty foul stuff.

I ordered beer, found it deliciously cold as beer always is in outback Australia, often the only evidence of any form of civilised living, and began tuning in to the talk around me, as is my habit.

Two pink men quite near me were having a conversation which was absurd, like most conversations in outback pubs by the time everyone has had five beers. The two of them were leaning on the bar peering earnestly into each other's deep-etched faces. Like two grotesque dolls, they carried on a nonsensical argument.

"He can."

"It'd kill him."

"It'd take four hours."

"It wouldn't kill him. Nothing would."

I leaned closer. Their voices were beginning to hit an hysterical note. Like buzzsaws, their shouts rose above the hubbub of the other drinkers. They were obviously used to yelling at one another fifteen metres underground with jackhammers going full blast.

"A hundred stubbies in four hours. Do you reckon that would kill him?"

"It'd kill anybody."

"He's not anybody."

They stared into each other's faces, the importance of the topic growing in their minds as the beer ran down their throats.

"Why are you so bloody sure?"

"Because I'm bloody sure."

One of them was almost middle-aged, with grey hair all over his exposed shoulders. At least, it would have been grey if he had washed off the pink dust. His face was dulled and brutalised by years of grubbing away in the ground all morning and drinking beer all afternoon. Or perhaps he had been born with a dull and brutal face.

His companion was younger, probably not thirty, a little fat but with the heavy shoulders and arm muscles of the opal digger. If men keep on digging in the ground for opal for a few generations, they will probably develop forequarters and arms like wombats. This younger man looked like a hairy-nosed wombat because of the three-day growth on his face. Not exactly like a wombat, though, because a wombat has some expression on its face if you look hard enough, while this character's face was just a blob of pendulous blankness. With its pink dusted stubble, it looked like a discarded serving of blancmange growing a strange mould.

"Well, if you're sure, will you bet on it?"

"Sure I'll bet on it."

You couldn't tell who was speaking because their voices sounded identical, like knives scraping on plates at an unbearably high volume. But you could tell the sound was coming from them and gradually a pool of silence was forming around them as the rest of the bar tuned into their conversation.

"What do you reckon, Ivan?"

Now you could see who was speaking because the older man turned and addressed himself to the drinker alongside him.

Ivan turned slowly and I realised I was looking at a monster. He stood barely a metre and a half high and was almost as wide across the shoulders. His chest, black-singleted and covered with dust, stood out like a giant cockerel's, a vast billow of muscles with dark streaks running over the pink dust as the sweat made its own little rivers. One great arm hung disproportionately low by his side, the other rested on the bar with an enormous pink hand almost totally concealing a glass of beer. His hair was short and closely cropped and he carried a comb of bristles over a face that for one mad moment made me wonder whether it is possible to cross a crocodile with a hippopotamus.

This was a face that displayed a complete lack of interest and malice, with a blank complacency that made it obvious no thought had ever disturbed the brain that nestled just under that absurd cockscomb of hair.

He was wearing shorts, and two massive legs, not unlike those of a hippopotamus except that they were pink and hairy instead of grey and wrinkly, propped up his body. It was as though the body was resting on the legs rather than being joined to them, because he seemed to have no waist; he was tree trunk-thick all the way down until suddenly he had legs. The junction was concealed by the baggy shorts, but I got the impression that the legs might walk away at any moment, leaving the body standing there.

"What do you reckon, Ivan? I reckon you could drink a hundred stubbies in four hours."

"'Course I could," said Ivan. His voice was flat and deep, almost pleasant by comparison with those of the other two, but only by comparison.

"There," said the older man, turning to his companion as though everything had been proven.

"Bet you he couldn't."

"Bet then. Go on, bet!"

"What do you mean, bet?"

"I mean what I say. What'll you bet he can't drink a hundred stubbies in four hours?"

"Bet you five hundred bucks."

The older man thrust his hand into his hip pocket and brought out a wad of notes. He counted ten fifties on to the counter. The younger man looked on impassively while Ivan, losing interest, turned back to his pint.

"Match that."

The younger man, having waited until the last fifty was laid down, dived into his own pocket and counted out his bundle of fifties. He paused before laying down the tenth.

"Who's paying for the beer?" he asked cunningly.

There was a long pause while this was pondered.

"Take it out of the centre," said the older man at last.

"All right, Ivan. Here's the biggest beer-up of your life, and on me," said the older man, grabbing Ivan by the shoulder.

"Come on, Bill," he said to the barman, "set up ten stubbies. Ivan's gonna sink a hundred."

Bill didn't react, just reached into the refrigerator and lined ten stubbies up on the counter.

"Off you go, Ivan. Remember, I'm betting on you."

"He's gotta be standing at the end," said the younger man, sullenly, now sounding worried.

"He'll be standing. Come on, Ivan. Sink 'em."

Ivan was looking at the ten stubbies. You could see he was thinking by the contortions on his face. You could almost hear him. The three men were now the centre of a large circle that had formed as the concept of the bizarre bet was grasped by the other drinkers. Money was appearing from dusty pockets as side bets were laid. Ivan was still thinking.

"Come on, Ivan."

"I want a hundred bucks," said Ivan.

The older man was shocked. "What do you mean, you want a hundred bucks?"

"I mean I want a hundred bucks."

"Whaffor?"

"Drinking the beer."

"But you're getting the beer free."

"I want a hundred bucks."

Conversations tend to be limited on the opal fields.

"You can go to hell."

"Right."

Ivan turned back to the bar and ordered another beer. The older man looked at this disbelievingly. Ivan downed his beer. Obviously he intended to stand by his position.

"All right then," said the older man desperately, "if you drink all of the hundred stubbies, I'll give you a hundred bucks."

"A hundred for trying," returned Ivan, without even turning around.

"God Almighty. What happens if you drink fifty beers and pack it in? Do I still give you a hundred dollars?"

"A hundred for trying," said Ivan.

The older man stared at the impossibly broad and unyielding back. You could tell that he was thinking, struggling for a solution. "Tell you what," he said finally, "a hundred and fifty if you make it, nothing if you don't. How's that?"

Ivan was thinking. A long pause. "All right," he said, and reached for the first stubbie.

"Take if off the top," said the older man to his companion, which presumably meant that the winner would have to pay Ivan's fee.

This seemed reasonable to the younger man, but he was slow to make up his mind. By the time he had nodded assent, Ivan had already drunk six stubbies.

His technique was impressive. He picked up one of the little squat bottles in each hand and flicked the tops off with his thumbs. Most men need a metal implement for this, but not Ivan, he had thumbnails he could use as chisels. Then he raised his right hand, threw back his head and poured the beer into his gaping mouth all at once, the whole bottleful, one continuous little jet of beer until the bottle was empty. Then he did the same with the bottle in his left hand. Both bottles empty, he put them down neatly on the counter and reached for two more.

There are 375 millilitres of beer in each of these bottles. Legally, if you drink three in an hour, you are too drunk to drive a motor car. One hundred bottles would be 37,500 millilitres. The mathematics are beyond me, but it must be a monumental weight of beer. I timed him. It took just on eight seconds to empty a bottle, one second to put the two bottles on the counter, one second to pick up two more, one second to flip off the tops. He was swallowing a stubbie every eleven seconds.

Swallowing's not the word. There was no movement in his throat. He was just pouring it straight down into his stomach. A stubbie every eleven seconds. At that rate, he would be able to drink 100 in 1100 seconds — that's less than an hour. But he couldn't keep that up. For obvious reasons; he'd burst, for one.

I wasn't the only man in the bar making these calculations. In the great circle that now surrounded Ivan, men were looking at their watches and counting. To save time the barman had put twenty cold stubbies on the counter just as Ivan downed the tenth. Ivan didn't pause. He was drinking, or working, as rhythmically as though he were on an assembly line: pour down one bottle, pour down the next, both bottles on the counter, pick up the next two, flip off the tops, pour down one bottle, pour down the next.

The only sound in the bar was the slap of the bottles on the counter and the metallic rattle of the bottle tops hitting the floor. All the drinkers were silent, watching in an almost religious awe, their own glasses held unnoticed.

I realised for the first time that the clock hanging above the bottles at the back of the bar had a chime. It chimed six o'clock just as Ivan finished his fortieth bottle of beer. As if it were a signal, he slammed the two bottles on the bar and paused. The silence became intense as everybody started leaning forward slightly, wondering. I was convinced Ivan would drop dead.

Ivan stood motionless, his hands on the bar, his body inclined slightly forward. The pause lengthened, the silence deepened, if silence can deepen. I could even hear the clock ticking. Suddenly, Ivan's back muscles convulsed and a monumental belch erupted through the bar, breaking the silence like a violent crack of thunder. I swear the front rank of spectators reeled back. There was a burst of cheering and laughing and clapping.

Ivan reached for the next two bottles and was back to his rhythm again. Forty-five bottles, fifty, fifty-five, sixty. The impossible was being translated into reality in front of our eyes. Then came a piece of virtuosity: Ivan flipped the tops of two bottles but instead of raising his right hand, he raised both hands and poured the contents of two bottles down his throat simultaneously. It took just eight seconds. Seven hundred and fifty milligrams of beer in eight seconds to join the flood that was already coursing through his stomach, intestines, bloodstream.

Technically he had to be dead. No human tissue could withstand an assault of alcohol like that. Perhaps Ivan wasn't human; perhaps he had never been alive. He had stopped again. He glanced around the circle of spectators.

"Had it, Ivan?" said one hopefully.

Ivan ignored him.

He looked to his principal, the older drinker. There was something he'd forgotten, a condition in the contract that hadn't been spelled out.

"Time out to leak?" he said, a little plaintively.

"Sure, get going," said his backer.

Ivan was away from the bar for five minutes, which wasn't surprising. I wondered whether he had regurgitated some of the beer, but this didn't seem to occur to anybody else.

At eighty bottles, Ivan stopped again. We waited expectantly for the mighty belch, but it didn't come. He paused for about fifteen seconds and then reached for two new bottles. But there was a change of pace. The mighty fingernails fumbled slightly before the bottle tops flew off. His movements were deliberate and ponderous. Once he missed his aim and a jet of beer splashed on to his chin. I wondered whether this counted as a whole bottle but nobody raised the point. He was pausing each time he set down the bottles.

I was aware that gently, almost whispering, the whole bar was counting: "Eighty-five, eighty-six, eighty-seven, eighty-eight." The count was slowing as Ivan's drinking rate slowed. By now he was taking fifteen seconds a bottle, then eighteen, nineteen. At ninety-five bottles, Ivan stopped again, one half-full bottle in his left hand. He leaned forward. We waited again for the belch, but there was no sound.

Ivan shook his head from side to side. I saw his eyes. They had gone completely white, like a blind man's.

Ivan started to sway.

"Come on, Ivan, into 'em, boy!"

Ivan's massive body swung around in a slow circle, his feet still firmly on the floor. But then he steadied himself and the giant hand was raised. But this time he put the bottle to his lips. It did not go down in one unbroken stream. He swallowed many times with great effort. He put the bottle on the counter and reached for two more. He couldn't get the tops off; the barman whipped them off for him. Slowly, painfully, his eyeballs rolled deep into his head, his body swaying in ever-increasing circles, Ivan drank each bottle.

"Ninety-nine!" It was a roar.

Then Ivan drank the ninety-ninth bottle. By then he was spinning quickly, inclining his body at an impossible angle. Only the weight and size of his legs can have kept him upright.

Somebody had to put the hundredth bottle into his hand. Obviously he couldn't see it, or anything else for that matter, but somehow his hand found his gyrating head and he got the bottle to his lips.

Down went the beer, slowly, terribly slowly. But down it went, all of it.

"One hundred!" It was a mighty animal scream. The empty bottle crashed to the floor. Ivan had drunk one hundred stubbies in just under an hour.

Three or four men tried to stop Ivan spinning and there was a general hubbub as bets were settled and fresh drinks ordered. Then Ivan brought instant silence with a vast bellow.

"Vodka!" he shouted.

The word, as much as the level of Ivan's thunderous voice, brought the silence.

He turned to the bar and thumped it.

"Vodka!"

Dazed, the barman poured him a nip of vodka.

Ivan brushed the glass off the bar with a sweep of his hand that demolished half a dozen other drinkers' glasses as well.

"The bottle!" he roared.

There was silence.

Then timidly, terrified in the presence of mystical greatness, the barman put a bottle of vodka on the counter. It was open, but Ivan broke its neck on the bar in a ritual gesture. Apparently he could see again, although his eyes were still just blank white.

He raised the vodka bottle until the jagged neck was a handspan from his mouth, then poured a gush of the clear spirit down his throat. Half the bottle gone, he slapped it down on the counter; it rolled on its side and the vodka slopped onto the floor. Nobody noticed.

Arms by his side, eyes pure white, body rigid, Ivan made for the door of the bar. A quick passage cleared for him and he went through in a stumbling rush, like a train through a forest. He crashed into the swinging door, the bright flash of late sunlight illuminating his huge frame, and plunged headfirst out into the street, hitting the dust with a thud that seemed to shake the building. Just once his head moved, and then he was a motionless heap of sweat-sodden humanity in the dust.

"We'd better get a truck to take the poor bastard home," said somebody.

"Yeah." And two of the drinkers, kindly men, wandered off to organise the truck.

"He's forgotten his money," said someone else.

"I'll keep it for him," said the barman. "He'll be back in the morning. Probably have a head."

# Tim Dooley
## Thomas E. Spencer

Tim Dooley lives down near the end of the town,
With his wife, and a horse, and a dray;
He'll fetch you a cartload of wood for a crown,
Or he'll go out to work by the day;
As a rule, Tim is one of the mildest of men,
And he drinks nothing stronger than tea,
But now and again something happens, and then,
Tim Dooley breaks out on the spree;
Then you hear the folks say:
"Quick! Get out of the way,
For Tim Dooley is out on the spree."

Then we hear a loud yell, that we all know full well,
'Tis a sound like a wild dingo's bray;
And the deafest old man in the township can tell
It is Dooley in search of his prey;
All business stops, for the folks close their shops,
Women snatch up their children and flee,
And the Methodist parson with fear almost drops,
When Tim Dooley gets out on the spree.
Our policeman turns pale,
And stops inside the gaol,
When he knows Dooley's out on the spree.

Now, the dread of a fray would not cause this dismay,
Or give rise to such panic and fear,
But who can his courage or valour display,
When he feels his last moment is near;
When Dooley gets tight he is mighty polite,
Wants to kiss everyone he may see,
And a whiff from his breath causes sure, sudden death,
When Tim Dooley is out on the spree;
So we hide, or we fly
When the rumour goes by,
That Dooley is out on the spree.

> "I rather like bad wine ... one gets so bored with good wine."
>
> BENJAMIN DISRAELI, 1845

# The Evenin' Before Leavin' Home
## Steele Rudd

It was drawing close to New Year when Sam Condle sent me word to get ready to go shearin' down the rivers with him an' some other chaps.

I was ready to go anywhere with anyone, not because there weren't plenty work about Vinegar Hill, but because Connie told me straight out one evenin' that she didn't want me comin' to see her any longer. An' after all th' conversation lollies I bought her, an' all the' wood I chopped for her too! By cripes, it made me furious.

"I'm off in th' mornin'," I sez to th' old lady. "An' might never come back to these parts again."

"Frankie, if I was you I wouldn't," she sez, with a terrible sad look on her.

Ah, an' when I think of how she coaxed an' coaxed me to stay, brings the tears to me eyes!

"Me boy, you are not strong enough to shear beside men as old as your father," she would say, "so wait till you get set an' have more practice."

Of course I didn't tell her about Connie, but I quoted Jack Howe shearin' his three hundred a day to her, an' reckoned if I couldn't hack me way through a couple o' hundred I'd eat me hat.

"An' th' terrible floods they have in them rivers," she went on, "carries horses an' men away; an' th' wild blacks. Oh, they'll massacre you all in th' night!"

I never heard anythin' before about blacks bein' down th' rivers, an' it made me hair stand up when she mentioned them.

"We'll give them all th' massacrin' they want, mother," I sez, treatin' it lightly, but at th' same time makin' up me mind to ask Sam how many there was down there.

"An' y' can't go without seein' your father," th' old lady continued, "there he is not over his birthday yet. Oh, th' terrible fool of a man that he is, an' gettin' worse instead of better every year. Where he'll find th' money to pay Dollar his wine bill when it's all over, I'm sure I don't know. This is no life for me an' your sisters to be livin', Frankie, an' if you're goin' to go away it will be far worse."

"He's been down there too jolly long, no doubt about that," I said, waggin' me head in agreement with her, and appearin' wise at th' old man's expense. "An' if he ain't home be eight o'clock tonight I'm goin' down to bring him."

"He might come for you," the old lady answered with a sigh, "but if I go near him there'll only be words, an' then he won't come at all."

When eight o'clock arrived, o' course th' old man wasn't home, an' down I goes to Dollar's.

Near Codlin's corner I sees a light comin' along th' road, an' hears a wheel squeakin', then a cove starts singin' loud an' another chap tells him to "hold his tongue". For a while I couldn't make out what sort of a trap they was drivin', but I could tell it was th' old man who was singin' be th' sort of "coo-ee" he used to begin the lines with. He always sung like a dingo howlin'. But when we got close together an' I sings out, "Hello!" they stopped. An' there was th' old man squattin' as comfortable as you like in a wheelbarrow with his back to th' wheel an' his legs danglin' over the back an' a lighted candle stuck on each side of him, an' a big square bottle o' wine in his arms, an' old "Scottie" nearly as screwed as himself in th' handles of th' barrow.

"By cripes!" I sez to them, "this is a nice sort o' thing."

"Thash you, Frankie?" sez th' old man.

"Of course it's me," I growled at him. "This is a nice sort of business; an' them sittin' up waitin' for y' at home."

"Yer needn't go down to (hic) Dollar's for me. I'm comin' home (hic) meself. Ain't we, Scot-(hic)-tie?"

"Aye, comin' home in (hic) Dollar's motor car, d' y' see, Frankie." An' raisin' th' handles of the barrow, Scottie proceeded to propel th' old man over stones an' ruts at a vigorous and reckless speed again.

I trotted along beside them actin' as a guide, an' thinkin' of the reception they would get from th' old lady when they reached home, an' silently wonderin' if all the horrors of drink wasn't more than compensated for be th' humours of it.

Every hundred yards or so Scottie would stop an' puff hard, an' tell th' old man he was as "heavy as yon German lassie i' th' wine (hic) shop".

"Take another drink," an' th' old man would hold out th' bottle to him. "An' make me a bit (hic) lighter for yourself."

Then Scottie would drink, an' off again.

Arrivin' at th' house th' old man broke into fresh song, an' th' dorgs begun barkin' an' th' old lady followed by th' girls come runnin' out. I knew they'd get a surprise when they saw him in th' barrow between th' candles like a blitherin' Chinese god. An' they got one too.

"I've brought him home to y' in a (hic) motor car, d' y' see," Scottie said to them, stickin' to the handles to keep himself from fallin'.

But they just stood starin' as if they had no tongues to talk with.

Last th' old man who kept blinkin' an' hiccupin' at them, an' thinkin' of th' blokes he saw givin' up their seats to ladies in th' tram th' time he took Fogarty's bull to th' exhibition, opens his mouth an' sez:

"You'll (hic) 'scuse me, ladies, for keepin' me (hic) seat."

Th' girls an' me bust out laughin', but th' old lady lost her block.

"You beast!" she shouted, an' grabbin' one of th' candles nearly burnt off his whiskers, with it. Then she kicked the barrow over, an' th' other candle went out an' old Scottie fell on top of th' old man an' they both started roarin' an' bitin' each other, an' I got ready to run. But seein' th' others wasn't frightent I waited too.

"A lovely pair! Two beautiful specimens of men! Come away, girls, come inside an' leave th' brutes."

An' carryin' what was left of th' bottle o' wine which she rescued when th' barrow went over, th' old lady bounced inside an' I after her.

Next mornin' first thing I rolled me swag up an' strapped it on th' pack horse along with a jackshay an' a pair o' greenhide hobbles that I made on purpose about three months before.

Soon as breakfast was over I grabs me hat an' sez, "Well, I got to meet th' rest of th' chaps at Hodgson's Creek in about an hour."

Then th' hand shakin' an' th' cryin' commenced, which was always the worst part o' going away. Anyone who's never left a home in th' bush don't know what that means.

"Look after y'self Frankie while you're away," th' old man who was the last to shake sez, "an' if ever ye see any drinkin' or gamblin' goin' on, keep away from it."

> "A bumper of good liquor
> Will end a contest quicker
> Than justice, judge or vicar."
>
> RICHARD BRINSLEY SHERIDAN, 1775

# The Atavism of Charlie Rednose
## Wilbur G. Howcroft

According to my uncle, Charlie Rednose was a drunken, lying, argumentative old reprobate. Furthermore, he was completely and utterly unreliable, with an aptitude for causing more trouble than a weasel in a henhouse.

The strange thing about it was that whenever Charlie took umbrage and left the farm after one of their frequent squabbles, Uncle would fret and complain over the old coot's absence until such time as Charlie condescended to reappear. This he always seemed to accomplish when least expected. Significantly, Uncle never employed another hand while Charlie was away, no matter how the work piled up.

Quite a character was this Charlie, a short, fiery-whiskered, scrawny-armed runt of a fellow, with the map of the world on his face and a curious habit of taking quick, furtive glances over his shoulder.

It seems he arrived humping his swag away back in the days when Uncle had finally got enough mallee rolled and burnt to broadcast and then disc in a few acres of wheat.

Together, apart from Charlie's occasional walkabouts, they ultimately cleared the whole block. Moreover, they fenced it, sank dams, built sheds, erected a rough *pisé* dwelling and performed all the backbreaking tasks then necessary to open up a new selection.

All this they did without a woman on the place to housekeep for them. Uncle remained a bachelor all his life. Marriage, he used to say darkly, was like shoving your hand into a bag of death adders in the hope of pulling out an eel.

As for Charlie, well, as he frequently pointed out, he could never afford sufficient booze and tobacco as it was, without wasting money on fancy clothes and tucker for a "long-haired mate"!

During school holidays I stayed at Uncle's whenever the opportunity arose. The free and easy life, in which one ate, slept and washed whenever one fancied, suited a youngster like me just fine. Happy memories of long evenings around the big, open, log-crackling fireplace with the men yarning and smoking their pipes remain with me to this day.

Uncle was cook; I don't recall Charlie frying as much as an egg. Uncle perpetually kept an enormous iron pot simmering on the stove, in which bubbled a heterogeneous concoction he always referred to as "stoup". I imagine he called it this because it was a mixture of stew and soup. Nevertheless, it tasted great to me in those days.

Charlie, however, occasionally raised his voice in protest about the "fodder", as he called it. "Damn it all, Jack", he'd growl to Uncle, "this blasted stuff's gettin' worse each flamin' week. Why, it tastes like a conglomeration of sawdust an' dead blanky flies!"

Once we dragged a dam before slushing it and netted several small English perch. Uncle gutted and fried them and we sat down to the eagerly awaited treat. Although Charlie cleaned up his portion before we had barely started ours, he nonetheless stoutly maintained he didn't enjoy it.

"Them ruddy fish are poor fodder," he observed, removing a few stray bones with two grimy, tobacco-stained fingers. "So 'elp me, it's like eatin' bloomin' cottonwool with pins in it!"

Of course, Rednose was not Charlie's real name: what that was I never did find out. Neither, to the best of my knowledge, did anyone else in the neighbourhood. According to district legend he acquired the second handle of his appellation through an alcoholic adventure that once befell him at a local race meeting. It appears that the old codger had been overcome by the demon drink to the extent that he flaked out in the wagon used to bring the barrels of beer to the booth. Moreover, he was still "wrapped in the arms of Bacchus" when the driver drove back to the hotel that evening.

A couple of local lads noticed the slumbering one and, after procuring some red enamel and a brush, carefully painted his nose. Some time later Charlie awoke with a raging thirst and blundered blindly about until he finally located the bar. He rushed in, "with his tongue hanging out like a rabid bulldog", as one onlooker later put it, and completely unaware of his wondrously eye-catching proboscis.

Charlie had a wonderful time that night. For some strange reason, entirely beyond his comprehension, virtually everything he said or did was greeted with hilarious acclaim by his appreciative audience. In fact, he discovered that merely to stand still and smile ingratiatingly sufficed to evoke gales of laughter and hearty thigh-slapping. Never before had he known such glory!

Next morning, as befits a man who has imbibed long and deeply, Charlie arrived late and bleary-eyed to breakfast, wearing the preoccupied look of one who has much on his mind.

Uncle, who had remained at home the previous day, took one incredulous look at his offsider's scarlet beak and nearly dropped the bowl of stoup he was carrying. "What the blazes have you been up to, you old goat?" he demanded. "You look like some mad demon king from a pantomime!"

"Dunno what you're talkin' about," Charlie retorted sourly.

"Just look at yourself, man!" roared Uncle, thrusting the shaving mirror in front of Charlie's face. "Go on, take a Captain Cook!"

Charlie started visibly, eyed his embellished snout speculatively for some moments, then remarked in matter-of-fact tones: "Well, fancy! I ain't had an attack o' that now in ages." He thereupon turned and, with all the dignity at his command, marched majestically outside.

The story of Charlie's red nose spread over the countryside like sugar in a bed, and was recounted with glee for years afterwards. As a consequence, it was almost inevitable that he should thereafter be known by the magnificently exclusive title of Charlie Rednose.

If there was one brag that Charlie indulged in above all others, it was his oft-repeated claim that he was descended from a long line of famous Scottish fighting men. "Yes," he would boast, "me ancestors were all celebrated warriors, renowned far and wide for their warlike ways and heroic deeds." He would then regale his listeners with hair-raising accounts of the various battles and massacres in which his bloodthirsty forefathers had allegedly taken leading roles.

"As for meself, though," he would hastily add, "I'm a man of peace and always try and act friendly to all folk." And then, by way of excuse for the ferocious doings of his forebears: "Of course, things were different in the old days."

Charlie was a firm believer in the doctrine of "turning the other cheek", and claimed that all disputes could be settled by talking things over. In support of this contention he constantly narrated sundry rather questionable anecdotes, all of which ended happily, solely because he had applied reasoning powers to the situation in place of brute force. His oratory on the subject was, at items, most impressive.

But one fateful day in the local pub, a stranger told a story that centred on the parsimonious character of the Scottish race. In the gale of laughter that followed, the nettled Charlie protested vigorously. With some heat, he denounced the allegation as being totally without foundation and suggested that, in the interests of harmony, a full retraction was called for.

"Garn," said the storyteller, coarsely, "all the Scotsmen I've ever known were that lousy they'd steal a fly from a blind spider."

At this dreadful effrontery, Charlie's face turned green and his eyes rolled in their sockets like billiard balls. Screaming some long-forgotten war-cry of his ancestors, he grasped a heavy drinker's stool and savagely clouted the stranger over the head, dropping him like a shot hawk.

Then, flinging himself upon his prostrate foe, he commenced pummelling him with such strength and tenacity that it took three strong men and the publican to pull him away.

Poor old Charlie was later ashamed of his lapse and was at a loss to understand the reason for it. Uncle, however, always maintained that Charlie's extraordinary behaviour could be explained by the fact that, at the time, a gramophone in the bar had been loudly playing bagpipe music. Maybe so ... who knows?

"Shearing sheep is dry work, kissing girls is sly work,
But drinking deep is my work; so drink, boys, drink."

ARTHUR PATCHETT MARTIN, 1882

# Bluey Brink
## Anonymous

There once was a shearer, by name Bluey Brink,
A devil for work and a demon for drink;
He'd shear his two hundred a day without fear,
And drink without blinking four gallons of beer.

Now Jimmy the barman who served out the drink,
He hated the sight of this here Bluey Brink,
He stayed much too late, and he came much too soon,
At evening, at morning, at night and at noon.

One morning as Jimmy was cleaning the bar,
With sulphuric acid he kept in a jar,
In comes Old Bluey a'yelling with thirst:
"Whatever you've got, Jim, just hand me the first!"

Now it ain't down in history, it ain't down in print,
But that shearer drank acid with never a wink,
Saying, "That's the stuff, Jimmy! Well, strike me stone dead,
This'll make me the ringer of Stevenson's shed!"

Now all that long day as he served out the beer,
Poor Jimmy was sick with his trouble and fear;
Too worried to argue, too anxious to fight,
Seeing the shearer a corpse in his fright.

When early next morning, he opened the door,
Then along came the shearer, asking for more,
With his eyebrows all singed and his whiskers deranged,
And holes in his hide like a dog with the mange.

Says Jimmy, "And how did you like the new stuff?"
Says Bluey, "It's fine, but I ain't had enough!
It gives me great courage to shear and to fight,
But why does that stuff set my whiskers alight?

"I thought I knew drink, but I must have been wrong,
For that stuff you gave me was proper and strong;
It set me to coughing, you know I'm no liar,
And every cough set my whiskers on fire!"

> "Give strong drink unto him that is ready to perish, and wine to those that be of heavy hearts."
>
> PROVERBS 31:6

# A Journalist's Funeral
## Anonymous (The *Bulletin*,1889)

It was a new sensation to be in a coffin, with a hearse all to myself as the sole passenger. I had exhausted all other sensations, and this seemed to be the last. Strangely enough I was not afraid, the utterly novel experience acted upon me like hasheesh. I actually enjoyed it in a dreamy contemplative kind of way. You will at once perceive that I was not dead at the time, or I would not be writing this now.

Two dismally shabby cabs crawled after my conveyance, and I noticed with mingled envy and indignation (so far as I could be touched by either of these feelings) that they stopped at every hotel on the road, in order that the mourners might have an opportunity of drinking my health, I suppose.

In the state of trance, for that was what it really was, in which I was at the time the mysterious faculty, sometimes vaguely called the sixth sense, must have been developed. I heard what my mourners were saying about me a plainly as if I had been sitting beside them, while the hearse went slowly grinding along the dusty road to the cemetery.

"He was nobody's enemy but his own — poor Jack!" said Mr O'Connell, blowing through the stem of his pipe to clear it. And out of the glass windows of the hearse, paid for, as I discovered afterwards, by a generous theatrical manager whom I have written slightly of on many occasions, but who, thank heaven, still survives to be repaid by my borrowing a tenner from him the first time we meet, I saw, through all intervening obstacles, this stout, dark little man making rings (mourning rings, I suppose) with his tumbler on the bar counter of the hotel.

And at once there flashed upon me a memory. It was a moonlit night in summer six years ago, ah, those happy days when I was so miserable!

I was on board one of the small steamers that run from Circular Quay to Mosman's Bay. Sitting beside me in a great grey coat which, with his head peering forward predaciously, so to speak, gave him the appearance of a bald-headed eagle, was the brightest and lightest writer I have met in these lands. He was not given to serious reflection as a general thing, and I was somewhat surprised when he turned to me suddenly and said in a tone of gloom so intense that it was almost grotesque: "They may say anything they please about me when I am dead, so long as they don't say 'He was nobody's enemy but his own'." And that is precisely what they did say, word for word. He has been dead for some years now, but his imitators have been many and one or two have almost succeeded in catching something of the ring of his style, reminding me of the tall skeleton in Goethe's ballad who is climbing up the steeple of a church to get at the sexton, and, when he has almost attained the top, falls to the ground, a heap of bones, the moment the cock crows.

We, that is to say, the hearse, the undertaker's men and myself, were about a mile ahead of my mourners just then. I noticed them coming out of the fourth public house on the road wiping their lips, and then the two disgraceful shandridans came tearing along, full gallop, after me. I also noticed that there was another funeral approaching by a cross street. There seemed to be no end to it. I remembered that it was the final procession of a prominent old pirate who had died a few days before me, and had been kept in state (on ice) till then. He had risen to affluence and a title by usury during six days of the week and carrying the plate around in churches on the seventh. He had most of the city following him to where he was going to sleep in hopes of a glorious resurrection. And I had only a wretched queue of two after *me*, a man of poetry and learning, a man who had hauled upon the Archimedean lever till it almost snapped with the strain! It was disgusting. If I could have only got out of my coffin and on to the box-seat of the hearse I would have made a vigorous dash, the processions being somewhat mixed, to divert the traffic and assume the lead of the retired pirate's cortége and let my two shabby cabloads go to mourn over *him*!

But they had overtaken us by this time, all talking together and smoking like chimneys.

"Well, there's no use crying over spilt milk, boys," (nobody was crying that I could see, so this must have been a mere *façon de parler*) said the sub-editor of the paper to which I used to contribute most of my work. "He's dead, and that's all there is about it. Brush away those tears!" (Spoken melodramatically, there were no tears.) "I've got to get out here to start on my work."

Which he at once proceeded to do, and went on his way with long strides and a slight lurch.

And this man I had considered a genuine, if not particularly demonstrative, friend of mine.

The miserable tail of two cabs, looking like desperate bailiffs on wheels, followed me until it came to the next pub. Then it detached itself again and the occupants shambled out. Presently a voice said, "Poor old boy! Here's luck to him wherever he goes. He was never afraid of hot weather."

"Not while there was any drink around," remarked Jim McCann, draining his pint of shandy gaff at one splendid swig.

"Plenty where he's going," said McNab, the commercial man, "he always liked his liquor hot."

And then this perjured calumniator of the dead began to tell a string of the most outrageous fictions concerning what he and I had done when we had been on "tears" together, things which, if they had ever happened, would have got us into gaol or the lunatic asylum half a dozen times over. Yet he actually intended these astounding fabrications as a tribute to my memory! It was his idea of a funeral eulogium.

"Well, gentlemen," said the first voice, "I must leave you here. I enjoy a spree as much as anybody, but I have some special work to do, and I can't neglect it. See the old boy planted truly and well."

And *he* went off. "Nice lot of heartbroken mourners *I* have," I thought.

My old friend Tom Dorgan, who had never said a word all this time, except that it was a fine day for a funeral, then observed, "The mourners are thinning out, Flynn."

"Yes," replied Flynn (a kindly cynic in his way), "they mostly do at the end of any funeral of this sort. You see" (it was an amiable characteristic of Flynn's that when he had an audience cooped up in a corner — and what better corner could be found than a mourning cab? He held that audience at his mercy, which wasn't much) "the poor old boy *had* to die. He didn't *time* his drinks, you know. All the time was his time when liquor was about" (another atrocious perjury), "and," jerking his thumb in my direction, "he has made all his time his own by it. Besides, the strain upon his intellect in writing comic paragraphs was enough to kill an emu. I'm beginning to feel it tell upon me, myself."

At this there was a muffled laugh, out of respect to the feelings of Flynn, I suppose.

"I want to get out at South Melbourne," said a husky voice from the corner of the cab.

It appeared that this gentleman had got into one of the cabs while the mourners and drivers were in a pub, saying what a fine fellow I was if I could only have kept sober one day a month or so, and being in a somewhat intoxicated condition, had mistaken it for one of the cabs that plied on the road to where he lived.

"I'd like to inform you, sir that you are at a funeral, and respect shall and will be shown to the illustrious dead, or there will be trouble," said McGinnis Walker, of the Press Bureau, for the first time. And with that McNab hustled the gentleman violently into the road. As soon as he had picked himself up he tore off his coat, threw his hat down, and challenged the entire funeral, offering to smash up the whole party and dance upon the corpse (regarding which he made certain coarse remarks that almost caused me to burst through my trance with rage).

But the funeral passed on and left him prancing around in a ring and defying everything within the circle of the horizon to come on and be ground into powder.

Soon after another mourner left. He said he would be late for dinner if he didn't get out at once and his wife would be very angry if such a tragedy occurred. And *he* departed.

"He was not a bad fellow, he was my best friend, boys, this has cut me up terribly. Have you got a match, Flynn?" said McNab, the commercial man.

"He stole two of my best original stories," growled McGinnis Walker, "but I forgive him, now he's dead. I stole them myself."

When we arrived at the grave there was only one mourner — McGinnis Walker, and he was asleep in a corner of the cab. All the rest had either got out or fallen out on the way. Tom had been overcome by his grief at the last pub, and McNab had been taken in charge by a policeman for offering in a public place to fight anybody who would dare to say that I wasn't the best all-round genius that had lived since the time of Shakespeare.

I felt three dull thuds on my coffin lid.

"Mother of Glory!" I yelled, "what's this?"

About a yard of the bedroom ceiling had fallen upon me.

I wonder if this will be anything like what will occur when I die? I don't care in the least so long as, in the words of my friend gone before, they don't say, "He was Nobody's Enemy but his Own."

> "I am prepared to admit some merit in every alcoholic beverage ever devised by the incomparable brain of man."
>
> H.L. MENCKEN, 1956

# Drinks With a Kick in Them
### Lennie Lower

The President of the Housewives' Association says that she does not believe in cocktail drinking and could, if necessary, produce a drink with a "kick" in it, from fruit.

Anticipating, we have evolved a few recipes to suit all tastes.

*Banana Flutter*
Take one banana, slice, and put into glass. Take half a coconut and beat it into a stiff froth. Mix briskly and serve. The "kick" is obtained by standing on one foot on the skin of the banana and leaning forward while pouring the drink down the back of the neck.

Then we have the *Flying Mule*
Take half-dozen raspberries, being careful to remove the seeds, also the sound. Mash lightly with hammer. Mix with little ice-water, and add seeds slowly, one at a time, until you are so thirsty that you'd drink anything. Now take a red-hot nail, and dip it smartly into the mixture, removing it almost immediately. Drink nail.

*The Watermelon Whoopee*
Take one large watermelon, cut in half. Hollow out one half and place contents in wash-basin. Save seeds from other half. Place in

wash-basin one small cup of gramophone needles, half-pint of sulphuric acid. Drink before bottom falls out of wash-basin.

A similar mixture is the *Hangover Blues*
The watermelon is put into the wash basin as before, but covered with crushed ice. The hollowed-out portion is then quarter-filled with crushed ice and placed over the head, taking care to pull it well down over the forehead. The face is then laid gently in the wash basin.

It will be seen from the above recipes that the uses of fruit as a drink are practically unlimited. Furthermore, most fruit is full of vitamines. These need not worry the hostess, however, as they can easily be detected by the small holes in the outside of the skin, and this part can be cut out.

And don't forget, all these drinks have a kick.

The careful hostess should warn her guests of this danger.

# A Song of Light
## John Barr

There have plenty songs been written of the moonlight on the hill,
Of the starlight on the ocean and the sun-flecks on the rill,
But one glorious song has never fallen yet upon my ear,
'Tis a royal song of gladness of the gaslight on the beer.

I have watched an amber sunset creep across a black-faced bay;
I have seen the blood-flushed sunrise paint the snow one winter
    day,
But the gleam I will remember best, in lingering days to come,
Was a shaft of autumn radiance lying on a pint of rum.

I have seen the love stars shining through bronze hair across my
    face,
I have seen white bosoms heaving 'neath a wisp of open lace,
But resplendent yet in memory, and it seemeth brighter far,
Was a guttered candle's flicker on a tankard in a bar.

# The Dark Ages

# Introduction

Here are stories concerning the physical and psychological results of drinking — the harsh realities.

Some of these stories are salutary tales which deal with the consequences of getting "roaring drunk": the hangovers, sufferings and recriminations of the regular binge drinker. Others are cautionary tales which explore issues like the social and personal cost of drunkenness, and the dreadful toll that alcohol exacts on individuals and society alike as a price for the temporary escapism it provides.

Some of these stories balance the horrors of intemperance with the humorous and farcical results of the drunkards' actions. In these stories we are invited to laugh at the misfortune and misery resulting from the drinker's over-indulgence.

Rarely have I read a more poignant description of a hangover than Lennie Lower's fine portrayal of the champagne headache endured by Jack Gudgeon the morning after his "good luck" at the racetrack. Here we are invited to enjoy the misery which the drinker inevitably brings upon himself.

In "The Lobster and the Lioness", however, we find ourselves laughing at the discomfort visited upon the "victims" of the inebriated Mr Thompson by his inadvertent act of befriending a lioness. The revenge he exacts upon the "wowsers" is even more enjoyable because it is unplanned and he has no awareness of it.

Other stories and verses here, like "There's a Patron Saint of Drunks" and "Doogan" examine more conventionally the results, consequences and inevitable realities of a drunkard's life. Perhaps the saddest of all these stories is Lawson's wonderful character sketch of a man lost to permanent brain damage from "DTs" in "Rats". For me the fact that Lawson and Dennis were alcoholics lends an extra piquancy and poignancy of their writings on the subject.

The blackest piece by far here, though, in my opinion, is "Nelly" which shows the effects alcohol can have when the person imbibing is devoid of any redeeming human features drunk or sober. The matter-of-fact narrative of this tale, written for the *Bulletin* over a century ago is as effectively chilling as it is ironic.

The sad manner in which society routinely deals with the effects of alcoholism and drunkenness is examined by Henry Lawson in "The Rising of the Court". It is the routine nature of court procedure which is really the most depressing aspect of the whole narrative.

Changing social conventions and trends in alcohol consumption are wickedly exposed and dealt with, in typical satirical fashion, by the incomparable Lennie Lower in "The Mixture As Never Before". Although he often wrote in praise of alcohol, and once called it "the last gift of the relenting gods", that never stopped Lower from satirising the social behaviour it initiated and the trendy suburban attitudes that surrounded its consumption.

In my own story here the character of Dipso Dan is an amalgam of many characters I have met and talked to over many years. I was taught to have respect and sympathy for drunks as a kid mainly because of a quirk of history. When I was a kid many drunks and "derelicts", as they were often called back then, were also "returned men", veterans of World War II or even World War I.

I am sure that a general awareness of the horrors of war and their effects on some "returned men" played a part in developing a tolerance of drunks throughout the 1920s and 1930s, and, after World War II, the 1950s. I developed some small understanding of the dreadful realities of a drunkard's day-to-day life by observing various "Dipso Dans" as a kid and later talking to them and getting to know them as a school teacher in small towns.

So these stories represent the darker side of drinking and alcoholism. Sure, some are amusing, others are written tongue-in-cheek and some use tall-tale exaggeration, but they all deal with the flip-side of the joy and release provided by drink which the stories in Section One explored.

Perhaps the sad reality exposed by these tales is that we are rarely, in this Australian society we inhabit, quite adequate human companions. We are mostly never imaginative enough, never sufficiently witty, never quite uninhibited enough to function without some aide or stimulant. So, we use the most socially accepted drug, alcohol, and we pay the inevitable cost both personally and socially. As Lawson said, "Beer makes you feel as you ought to feel without beer."

> "Drink, drink, drink, seems to be the universal motto, and the quantity that is consumed is incredible; from early morning to dark night — Bacchus being constantly sacrificed to."
>
> REV. J.C. BYRNE, 1847

# Champagne After the Races [from *Here's Luck*]
## Lennie Lower

The waiter coasted down to our table and pulled up with the silence of a Rolls-Royce hearse.

"Yessir?"

"A bottle of champagne, waiter," ordered Stanley.

"Two bottles," I put in.

The waiter's eyes glistened.

"Three bottles!" declared Stanley.

"Four no-trumps!" cried the waiter.

We stared at him.

"Sorry, sir," he stammered. "Pardon — forgot myself. Three bottles. Yessir."

Stanley tapped his forehead as the man hurried away.

"Bridged," he muttered pityingly; "probably from birth."

I nodded. I had seen too much of that sort of thing to pity the man. In the early days of my married life Agatha had threatened to divorce me for failing to lead the ten of diamonds. By some outrageous whim of a malicious fate we subsequently won the rubber and she stayed with me. I have never played the game since.

The champagne enlivened me. It thrilled and uplifted me like the fangs of a bull-ant. Champagne is another symbol of achievement. It puts a laurel wreath back among the rest of the shrubs. If headaches were created for any practical purpose, it was to show the glory of champagne. To emphasise the beauty of the rose by the magnitude of its thorns. And we had five bottles altogether.

It was with great difficulty that the waiter and I managed to carry Stanley out to a taxi some time later. It would have been easy, only the fool waiter, muddling round with his end of Stanley, made me lose my balance and fall to the floor several times before reaching the footpath. The man was obliging enough and I gave him a handful of pound notes as some slight recompense for his trouble, urging him at the same time to bank some. He offered to go in the taxi with us and wanted to brush me down. I couldn't stand for the brushing down. Positively couldn't stand for it.

We left the restaurant, with the waiter standing in the doorway gazing sadly after us, as though he had missed an opportunity to relieve his fellow-men.

I forget how we got home, and how it came about that we both decided to sleep on the doormat instead of in bed. Probably it was a hot night. I do not indulge in the stupidity of cluttering up my mind with the memory of insignificant details and I am unable to remember anything about it. The milkman disturbed me in the morning and I had hardly snuggled back on to the mat when the man who delivers the morning papers struck me in the ear with a deliberately aimed *Herald*. By the time the postman arrived Stanley was awake and I sent him to the gate for the letters. There were three of them and, as a number of female broadcasters in the terrace opposite were hanging out of their windows like dogs' tongues, we retired into the house before opening the letters.

Stanley flung them on the kitchen table and we sat down. Only one was addressed to me and that was from the Easy Payment Company. Easy payment; the savage irony of the term!

It was a final notice to the effect that they would remove the gramophone if payment was not made within seven days. I filed it away among the other final notices, wondering why the postman had bothered to deliver the thing. Perhaps the drain was full. I resolved to speak to him about it.

I chewed my fingernails and looked across at Stanley. He was looking at me and holding his forehead on with both hands.

"Here," I said, "go and get five pounds' worth of aspirin tablets for yourself."

His mouth flickered in a feeble smile.

"Aw, gee! Yes. Aspirin tablets." He pulled himself to his feet and plodded to the door.

"Aspirins!" he gasped, fumbling with the handle.

The telephone bell rang with a piercing tingle that set my brains beating against my forehead.

Stanley groaned, and staggering to the phone lifted the receiver off. "Oh, go on," he moaned in a stricken voice.

A moment of silence.

"Oh, Daisy! Oh, I'm splendid, thanks. Dad? Yes. He's in the kitchen. I'll call him."

"I'm not in!" I shouted.

"Hello. He's not in. Yes, he was in the kitchen a while ago. Yes. Call him a bit later. Good-bye."

He dropped the receiver on the floor and dragged his feet toward the front door.

"Going out, Stanley?" I called.

"I think so," he replied weakly. "I'm flickering."

The door slammed behind him and I pressed my forehead against the gas stove. The touch of the cold metal was like the hand of a faith-healer. It was uncomfortable kneeling on the floor with my head to the stove, so I lifted the door off it and carried it into the bedroom and lay down on it.

> "The temperate man sees the same world always, the proper inebriate finds the world never presents the same aspect twice."
>
> DAVID IRELAND, 1971

# The Lobster and the Lioness
## Ernest O'Ferrall

At eleven o'clock Thomson, who had broken his glasses during a last whirling argument re the chances of the Liberal candidate, was pushed gently out the side door and told to go home.

Instead of taking the barman's advice, he sat on the horse trough, holding the lobster he had bought for his supper wrapped in newspaper, and held an indignation meeting with himself until Sergeant Jones happened along.

"Goodnight, Mr Thomson," said the sergeant kindly.

Thomson pushed his hat to the back of his head. "Good evenin'," he returned sulkily.

"Are ye comin' down the street?" ventured the sergeant.

"Cert'nly not!" said Thomson. "I've lost me glasses, an' me eyesight's 'stremely bad. I can't see what I'm doin'!"

"Well, come along and walk with me. I'll see ye as far as the gate."

Thomson rose unsteadily, "I tol' you before I've broken me glasses. Do you mean to 'sinuate I'm *drunk*?"

"I do not!" said the sergeant. "I never saw a soberer man in my life! But come along now, an' I'll tell ye somethin' I heard today about Prince Foote f'r th' Cup. I'm goin' your way!"

On those honourable terms Thomson condescended to take up his lobster and allow Jones to pilot him gently toward his lodgings.

According to Thomson's reckoning, they had trudged through 283 deserted streets and turned 1834 strange and unexpected corners, when he found they were both standing still on a vacant piece of land, in front of an enormous board with "For Sale" on it.

"Wasser matter?"

"I heerd a strange sound," answered the sergeant. "Be quiet a minit! Maybe we'll hear it agin!"

They waited breathlessly.

A deep, muffled grunt arose close by.

"That's it!" said the sergeant excitedly.

"Somebody's drunk," sighed Thomson wearily. "Sailor prob'ly."

The sergeant snorted. "No sailor ever made a sound like that! Look, it's gettin' up! Is it a dog? ... *Run, man! Run for your life!*" he yelled, and ran heavily up a dark lane.

Thomson, swaying on his feet, patted his leg and called encouragingly to the approaching thing, "Goo' dog!"

Two yellow eyes glowed in the darkness.

"Goo' dog!" cooed Thomson encouragingly, and patted his leg again.

A deep, hungry growl.

"Come on, ole feller. I won't hurt yer!"

The thing with the smouldering yellow eyes came a step nearer, and Thomson cried out in delight, "By George! That's th' finest mastiff I've ever seen! I'll get him to foller me back to th' boarding-house!" He staggered off sideways, murmuring endearments, and stopping every few yards to flick his fingers or pat his leg. And the escaped circus lioness followed him as if he had been another Daniel.

They went slowly up the long, flat street that stretched away to a plain of burnished silver, the sea. The moon had slipped from her cloud dressing room and was hurrying down the sky like a woman going in search of a policeman.

Thomson staggered on, hugging his lobster, until he reached a lamp-post. Then he sat down, and calling affectionately to the lioness, started to eat. "Here ye are, ol' boy," he cooed. A claw hit the lioness on the nose and dropped to the pavement. The beast growled at the indignity but ate the fragment, and licked her chops with evident pleasure.

Thomson methodically dissected the food with his hands and chewed stolidly, occasionally throwing a bit over his shoulder with a mumbled word of encouragement. The lioness sat on her haunches and growled between courses, but accepted the scraps with a sort of eager humility. This went on till the lobster was no more. Thomson then wiped his mouth with the back of his hand, leaned against the lamp-post and closed his eyes. In a minute he was asleep. In another thirty seconds, he gave a long, whistling snore like the wail of a distant siren.

The wild beast, sitting erect like a thing of stone, growled nervously.

Thomson snored again.

The lioness growled angrily.

Thomson awoke with a start. "Who said that?" he demanded. "Who denies that Wade's done more f'r th' country than th' blanky Labor party — *eh*?" He turned slightly and beheld the enormous beast. "Goo' dog!" he cooed. "Goo' dog!"

Faintly, from the distant sea of city lights, came the clear chimes of a clock, followed by twelve, deep solemn notes. Brother timepieces to right and left answered it like watchful guardians of the hours.

Thomson rose slowly with a look of determination and flicked his fingers. "Come on, ol' boy! Mus' be gettin' home!" He staggered along for about twenty yards, and the lioness, her head down and her tail straight out, tracked him step by step. Then he paused. The beast stopped dead, with her glowing, yellow eyes fixed on his face. Thomson didn't notice her; his mind was grappling with some tremendous problem. "Where did I leave it?" he moaned at last. "I'll go back an' look!" With tremendous care, he steered a wavering course back to the lamp-post, moored himself to it, and peered all round the circle of light. The thing he sought was nowhere to be seen. "Dammit! I wonder where I lef' that lobster? … I'm certain I had it — an' I can *smell* it now! … Somebody's done me for it!"

Far up the street, approaching bootheels made a clear, crisp clatter in the still night. "I'll ask this chap if he's seen it!" murmured Thomson, and took a firmer grip of the post.

The lonely pedestrian came up rapidly and proved to be a slight young man in evening dress.

Thomson raised his hat. "'Scuse me, did you notice a 'stremely large lobster as you came 'long?"

The stranger stopped dead, stared past Thomson into the gloom beyond, and, with a muffled cry of horror, turned in his tracks. He ran with amazing swiftness into the night.

"Hol' on!" yelled Thomson after him, but there was no answer, merely the sound of a man running.

The lobster-loser turned disconsolately and found the lioness looking intently in the direction the stranger had taken. "Served him right if I sooled th' dog on him!" he reflected bitterly. Then, with an air of resignation, "Come on, Carlo, ol' boy; if coffee-stall's open, I'll get a pie." Once more he set sail, and the immense beast of prey followed stealthily in his footsteps at a distance of three paces.

Down the road they went, round two corners and across an unoccupied grassy lot, then along a dark, shop-lined street. At the far end near the kerb gleamed the headlights of a coffee stall. As Thomson drew near the proprietor was seen leaning on the counter, absorbed in reading by the light of his big lanterns, the account of the previous night's fight.

Out of the darkness a command came to him: "Hey! Give's a pie an' 'nother f'r th' dog!"

The proprietor looked up cheerily. "Right-oh!" He put down his paper and turned to fill the order. As he opened his oven door a delicious whiff of hot meat perfumed the frosty air. The lioness in the shadow growled loudly.

"'Oo did *that*?" asked the hot-pie man suspiciously.

"Sorright," Thomson assured him; "th' dog won't hurt yer."

"Wot sorter dorg *is* it?" persisted the pieman, vainly endeavouring to see what species of animal was beyond the light.

"Mastiff," explained the amateur lion-tamer wearily. "Prize mastiff — mos' 'fectionate beast. Gimme two pies!"

The pie artist extracted two of his finest works from the oven and placed them on the counter just as the lioness growled hungrily again.

"Better give us another pie f'r th' dog," said Thomson, putting a shilling down on the counter, and taking up one of the bandboxes of nourishment.

The coffee-stall man ignored the order, and, leaning far over the counter, looked into the shadow. His eyes bulged with apprehension. "*That* ain't no mastiff," he breathed at last. "It looks more like a — *gorstruth*!" With one mad bound he was over the counter and away. Thomson howled after him indignantly, and waited for five minutes to see if he would come back.

He didn't.

At last, Thomson climbed carefully over the counter, threw two sizzling pies to the lioness, and recommenced on his own. Fortunately the lioness's share fell into the gutter, and was thereby cooled, otherwise tragedy would probably have happened then and there.

After the light refreshments had been consumed, Thomson climbed down and invited Carlo to follow him again. Some blind instinct guiding his feet, he at last came by devious ways to the terrace house where he wasn't a star boarder.

Hanging on to the frost-cold railings in the moonlight, he communed with himself thus: "If I take th' dog roun' back, I'll wake up all th' dogs in th' place and fall over dust-bin. Let's see! … Yes, I better take old Carlo in fron' door and go through house. That's it! That's what'll do. Come on, ol' chap!"

With extreme care and patience he at last found the keyhole and flung wide the door. Then he lit a match and cooed encouragingly, but in vain, until the flame burned his fingers.

"*I'll* get him in!" he muttered, and, stumbling through to the kitchen, he found a large piece of raw steak. After opening the back door, he returned to the front and waved it at the lioness.

"Come on, Carlo!" he commanded. The beast, growling slightly, started to follow him. He backed into the hall, intending to lure his prey right through; but she was too quick for him. At the foot of the stairs she darted forward and snatched the steak from his outstretched hand.

"Give it here, damn yer!" he hissed, and made a wild grab at the goods.

The brute snarled horribly, and thumped the floor angrily with her heavy tail. Thomson staggered back and his match went out.

A door on the first landing opened explosively, the wavering light of a candle illumined the upper part of the staircase, and a quavering soprano voice cried, "Is anyone there?"

"Sorright. It's only me!" replied Thomson irritably. "I've gotter dog!"

The candle, a wrapped-up head and a long thin arm appeared over the banisters. "Do you mean to say you are bringing a dog through the *house*, Mr Thomson?"

"It won't hurt th' damn house!" retorted the bringer-home-of-lions, staring upward defiantly.

"Mr Thomson," chattered the partially hidden landlady, "you are not in a fit state to argue. I will speak to you in the morning!" The hand that held the candle shook with rage, and, as a natural consequence, the light wavered considerably.

"I *am* fit t' argue, and I *will* argue 'slong as I please! An' what's more, I'll do what I damn well please in th' rotten house, and bring as many dogs as I want inter it! Why, yer know yerself it's only fit f'r dogs! Come on, Carlo, ol' chap!"

He made a grab at the lioness's head but missed. The brute snarled again, louder than the largest-sized dog.

"If you have any respect for yourself," wailed the landlady, "I say if you have any *respect* for yourself, you will take that bloodthirsty brute out of the house!"

"Gorrer bed!" shouted Thomson. "Gorrer bed, an' mind yer own bizness, you — you *ole meddler*!"

"How *dare* you!" shrieked the landlady, and fled horror-stricken to her room.

Then, alone and unseen in the hall, Thomson performed a really fine taming feat. Lighting his second last match to see what he was doing, he walked behind the lioness and gave her a hearty kick. "*Gerrout!*" he yelled and the lioness, with an ugly shriek, ran lightly down the hall, and out into the yard. Thomson then shut both doors, back and front, and stumbled heavily upstairs to his room, where, without troubling to undress, he climbed solemnly into bed.

On the stroke of three he awoke and muttered, "Warrer! I wonder if warrer-bottle's been filled." He struggled sadly out of bed, and blinked at the wash-stand, dimly visible by the light of the waning moon. He could not make out a water bottle, but something white and round like a china bowl gleamed invitingly by the wash-basin. "I dunno what's in it, but I'll drink it, whatever it is!" he sighed, and made dry-mouthed for the waiting refreshment. He seized the bowl, and conveyed it half-way to his lips, then dashed it to the floor. It bounced lightly under the bed. "*Blast th' collar!*" he shouted, and started to fumble for matches. He persevered nobly until the water-jug meanly bumped against his elbow and smashed with a terrific sound on the floor.

"That settles it!" he said, and plumped down on the bed. "I'm not goin' to' degrade meself by gettin' drink for meself in soap-dish!" For five wrathful minutes he sat and savagely wondered how best to revenge himself. Finally he opened his room door and bawled: "Where's my shavin' water?"

The landlady's door flung open and she appeared on the threshold, done up like a sort of original mixture of Lady Macbeth and the Worst Woman in Sydney after a gas explosion. "How *dare* you?" she cried tragically. "What do you *mean* by asking for shaving water at this hour?"

Thomson, not at all abashed, lurched to the lobby railings, and leaned over like a candidate addressing an election crowd from the balcony of an hotel. "What do I want *warrer* for? *I'll* tell yer why! *I want t' drink it!!* I've decided t' reform and join th' No-Licence crowd. I'm goin' t' be a Wowser! I think pubs are curse to *ev'ry* man! If there were no pubs, you'd have t' keep beer in th' house, and we wouldn't have t' go *out* f'r it. D'ye understan' that, missus? D'yer see?"

"You forget yourself, sir!" trumpeted the landlady.

"I wish *you* wouldn't forget t' put warrer in my room! It's all damn fine t' gas 'bout 'totalism, but why don't you s'ply some warrer? Has warrer gone up?"

"This is too much!" wailed the wretched landlady.

She turned and tapped sharply with her bony knuckles on the door of the next room, and a sleepy male voice said: "All right! Be there directly."

Thomson leaned far over the railings and sniffed suspiciously. His nose wrinkled in disgust.

"Who's keepin' bears?" he demanded excitedly at last. "I'm not goin' t' stay in this place if you're goin' t' take in bears!"

"You are drunk!" chattered the landlady furiously. "How *dare* you say there are animals in the house?"

Thomson sniffed again. "Why, th' house stinks like a circus! It's bears, or tigers, or somethin'!"

The landlady raised a shaking hand, and pointed an accusing finger at him. "If there is anything in the house you brought it in yourself!" she intoned.

The door of the other room opened, and a tall, thin spectacled man, in a purple dressing-gown, stepped out. "What is all the noise about?" he inquired bitterly, holding his candle on high like the Torch of Liberty.

"I say that there's *bears* in th' house!" repeated Thomson.

The tall man inhaled deeply. "There certainly is a strong odour of animals," he remarked acidly.

"What did I tell yer?" cried Thomson triumphantly. His voice rang through the house, and two more doors were heard to open slightly.

The tall, embittered man turned to the landlady. "I suppose, Mrs Tribbens, Mr Thomson has brought home a monkey or something of the kind. He seems to be able to do just as he pleases in this house. I dare say we shall become used to the smell in time; but I really must object to being called up in the middle of the night to talk about the matter. Surely it would have done in the morning!"

"You don't understand, Mr. Pyppe," retorted the landlady with fearful hauteur.

"No, I'm afraid I don't," said Pyppe irritably. "The whole thing seems ridiculous to me. Why on earth I should be called out of bed at this hour of the night to talk about an unpleasant smell with a man who is obviously ..."

*Crash!* The tinkle of glass falling on stone told the landlady that the kitchen window had succumbed.

"*What's that?*" she gasped. Down the pitch-dark hall they heard sounds which suggested a burglar in stockinged feet dragging the body of a murdered boarder over the linoleum.

"I will see what it is!" Pyppe announced in a loud voice, and went cautiously downstairs, a step at a time.

Thomson and the landlady stared after him.

"*Who is there?*" cried the brave investigator, holding his candle far out over the railings.

There was no answer.

"*Who is there?*" he snapped. His candle tilted and a drop of hot wax detached itself and fell into the well of gloom. A grating, bestial roar of rage rang through the place, and a lithe, yellow animal sprang into the lighted radius and stood lashing its tail.

"*My God, it's a lioness!*" shrieked Pyppe, really shaken for the first time in his life. His candle clattered from his hand, and he rushed upstairs into his room and slammed and bolted the door.

"I *tol'* yer so!" shouted Thomson exultantly outside the landlady's door, from behind which came hysterical sobs and the shrieking of castors. "I *tol'* yer there was bears in th' house!"

"The police!" wailed the distracted woman. "The telephone! Ring for the police!"

"I give you me notice now," continued Thomson, above the sounds of hurried barricading. "I think it's disgustin'! *Why, your damned lion might have eaten my dog!* I'm going t' leave t'morrer, d'ye *hear*? I'm not goin' t' live with lions! I'm *sick* of yer stinkin' house!"

A deep, menacing growl floated up the staircase.

Thomson sprawled over the rails. "*Shurrup!*" he commanded, and the lioness, absurdly enough, was still. "Stinkin' brute!" he muttered without the slightest sign of fear, and made for the telephone on the landing.

In a minute or so he had the police station, and was speaking: "That th' p'leece station? Yesh. Well, this is Thomson speakin' here. Eh? Yesh, Thomson, of Gladstone Manshuns (*I dont' think!*). Can you hear? … I say, there's a lion in th' hall here waitin' t' be fed … Eh? … Yes, a *lion!* … No, I'm wrong, ol'chap — it's th' lion's wife. Are you there? … Well, it's waitin' to' be fed. I dunno who it b'longs to, but I'm goin' t'leave in the mornin'. It's stinkin' th' place out. Eh? … *What's* that? … Yesh, Gladstone Manshuns — you know th' place near th' Town Hall! Eh? … No, nobody's killed; there's nothin' here t' eat but boarders, never is! Are you comin' along? … Right-oh!" The bell tinkled hurriedly in the darkness. Thomson fumbled his way into his room and shut the door.

It was a lovely, peaceful morning. There wasn't a sound until two policemen and a little man, in the ring-costume of a tamer, trotted round the corner.

Thomson waved frantically to them from his window. "Go roun' side an' get in th' scullery window!" he howled. "Look out f'r my dog in th' backyard, he's big mastiff, but he won't hurt yer. If he growls give him a bit o' lobster, he loves lobster!"

> "Poor drunks, sore drunks — heads as big as tanks,
> Drunks that keep the town alive with their funny pranks;
> Glad drunks, mad drunks, yellow drunks and white —
> Somehow I meet a lot of drunks whenever I get tight."

"SYD SWAGMAN",1927

# There's a Patron Saint of Drunks
## Jim Haynes

There's a patron saint of drunks. Someone looks after them. It's almost impossible for a drunk to hurt himself and it's very difficult to get the better of a drunk.

I'm not really talking here about part-time drunks or weekend drunks. I'm talking about genuine drunks, those who make a vocation of being drunks, whose character is defined by the fact that they're drunks. We had a few like that in Weelabarabak but the most memorable of them all was the "town drunk" for many years, Dipso Dan.

His real name was, I believe, Daniel Harvey. The whole town, however, referred to him as "Dipso Dan", and to his face he was called either just "Dan" or "Dipso".

Dipso Dan wasn't born in Weelabarabak. Like most town drunks I've known he drifted into town from somewhere else, found a place to camp, did a bit of casual work now and again and got on with the job of being the town drunk. It was rumoured that he had grown up in Melbourne and come to the bush as a sideshow worker. He'd even fought in boxing tent shows many years ago and was "pretty handy" according to some of the older blokes around town. Old Nugget reckoned he remembered him going a few rounds with some of locals many years ago at the Weelabarabak Show, when he was a regular member of King Riley's Travelling Boxing Show.

As the grog slowly got to Dipso he had slipped down the carnival pecking order, becoming a rigger and a "rousie" and eventually, when he couldn't perform any regular productive work, he had been left behind in Weelabarabak to become our town drunk.

Dipso wore old woollen army pants tied with rope in place of a belt, a flannel shirt of an indeterminate shade and shoes that varied in type and colour depending on charity. I remember that he never wore socks and his old army pants ended about six inches above his shoes, revealing a fair bit of bony shank. He was always accompanied by his dog, Digger.

Dipso was a fairly happy drunk though he could be an absolute pain in the neck if you were trying to have a couple of quiet ones and a bet at the Tatts on Saturday. He always tried to tell you yarns about his illustrious punting career and wanted to know if you had "a good thing in the next". But there was no malice in Dipso; he wasn't a "fighting drunk" in spite of his reputed past career in the ring. He was painfully thin and seemed incredibly uncoordinated for an ex-boxer. He moved with a strange, jerky dancing motion that I found fascinating when I was a kid. Perhaps it was a combination of his boxing days dancing around the ring and the effect of years of booze.

One year the famous Tintookies Marionette Theatre came to Weelabarabak and put on a show. The whole school was marched down to the CWA hall and sat on mats at the front, near the stage, while the adults who weren't working sat in chairs behind us. The show was a ripper too, although I don't remember the plot or the characters very well. What everyone in town does remember is what happened when the curtain opened. The first marionette, a swaggie character, appeared on stage. The strings that operated the puppet gave it that jerky walking action that marionettes have. Half the kids on the infants and junior school mats called out in unison, "It's Dipso Dan!" It almost brought the show to a standstill.

The poor puppeteers must have wondered what these kids were yelling about. They no doubt also wondered why the adult audience was in stitches before the action had even begun. I bet they thought we were a very odd lot and were pleased to move on to the relative civilisation of Coopers' Junction for their evening performance.

Us kids used to imitate Dipso quite a bit, especially after we saw the marionette theatre performance. Kids are pretty insensitive and cruel and although Mum warned us that it was wicked to make fun of drunks like old Dan, my cousin Gerald and I used to pretend to be Dipso whenever we had creaming soda, a soft-drink that developed a creamy head like beer if you shook it up before pouring it.

Dipso was always getting barred from the Tatts. He had even been barred from the Royal a couple of times, which was pretty rare. He didn't mind that too much; publicans changed fairly regularly at the Royal and they were always desperate for customers, so Dan wasn't usually barred for long. What did terrify Dipso was the thought of being barred from the Royal by Dot the barmaid while he was still barred from the Tatts by Dougie.

Dipso lived in mortal fear of Dot, who worked most of the evening shifts at the Royal. If he was barred by Dot he had to rely on getting a sneaky drink from Happy Harold at the Royal before Dot came to work. This meant his evenings would be very dry and lonely affairs. It was rumoured that, under these circumstances, Dipso drank metho down in his camp near the river.

I know for a fact that this was more than a rumour because of a conversation I had with Dipso one Friday afternoon at the Tatts. I must have caught him at the very start of a bender because he was quite articulate.

"How's a boy?" he asked. Dipso always slurred his words slightly and his head, arms and shoulders were never completely still when he spoke. You got used to it after a while but it could be very disconcerting at first. He also spoke with a constant slight hesitation that never quite became a stammer. "Got a winner for t … termorrer?"

"No, Dan, haven't even had a look at the form yet," I answered.

The trick was to be polite, not make eye contact, and hope he'd move on. It worked maybe one time in every three, but not that afternoon.

"Well, you t … tell me when you've p … picked one," he said, patting me on the shoulder. "And how about making an old digger happy and buying me drink?"

"You're not an old digger, Dan," I replied, trying to keep my head in the paper.

"I know that," Dipso chuckled, "but I got a d … dog called D … Digger and he'd be happy if you bought me one." He could be quite funny sometimes.

So I bought him a seven-ounce glass of beer and he told me about his recent troubles with Dot and Dougie. "Trouble was I think I p … peed me pants on the carpet and Dougie hates that," he confided to me. "I'm glad he's let me back in anyhow, a man could end up drinkin' metho!"

"Well Dan, things aren't that crook yet," I said. "Anyway, I don't know how anyone could actually *drink* metho."

"Well it's not easy," he replied, "you need a t … terbacca tin and you pour it in real shallow and mix it with condensed milk or s … soft drink cordial mix, or boot polish if that's all you've got, then you can usually get it down."

I was stunned by the matter-of-fact nature of this reply. "Strewth, that sounds bloody awful Dan!" I said.

"Well it t … tastes worse than it sounds too," he assured me, "but it's even worse if you've got nothing to go with it, then you have to light the fumes and drink it out from under them —

straight from the t … terbacca tin." Dipso went on to tell me all the names metho had when mixed in different ways. It was "white lady" when mixed with condensed milk, "red" was the boot polish mix — and there was more that I've forgotten and thankfully never needed to remember!

That conversation changed my attitude to Dipso Dan quite dramatically. I didn't mind buying him the occasional beer once I knew something about the alternatives. I even offered him a lift home once or twice, but he told me he was "orright" and said the sergeant usually got him "back to camp" if he couldn't manage it himself.

Dipso's camp was an old shack down on the river just out of town. Between "benders" in town he lived there with Digger. Dipso told me dogs were great to talk to when you were drunk and "no other bastard would talk to you". He had Digger from when I was a teenager until long after I left town. Digger was a little brown kelpie that Old Nugget had given him as a pup. He was out of Nugget's good working bitch but was born a runt with a deformed back leg, so Nugget gave him to Dipso for two reasons. Firstly, Dipso had just lost his previous dog to a brown snake down at their camp. Secondly, it meant Nugget didn't have to "hit the poor little bugger on the head" — Nugget was very soft-hearted for an old bushman.

Digger followed Dipso everywhere and always waited for him outside the pub. Digger was much more popular around town than his master. All the kids would pat him as they passed the pub and my Uncle Lennie used to feed him regularly at the back of the fish and chip shop.

At least Digger ate regularly. Dipso wouldn't eat at all when he was on a bender. Sometimes he didn't get home for days at a time. He'd sleep in Anzac Park or at the back of whichever pub he got thrown out of at closing time, with Digger to keep him warm. If someone caught him up and about before the pub opened Dipso might be offered something to eat, I think Uncle Lennie fed him occasionally at the back of the fish and chip shop, as well as Digger. Mostly, though, he'd drink for days at a time and then either get some provisions at the general store (a few loaves of bread and tins of camp pie which he'd share with Digger) and go home to dry out for a while, or he'd put himself in the lock-up, if the sergeant hadn't already put him in there for being drunk and disorderly.

Often Mrs Sayer, the sergeant's wife, would discover Dipso in the cell when she went to clean up in the morning. "Did Bill put you in there or did you put yourself in, Dan?" she would ask.

"I put meself in, missus," Dipso would reply, "I'm real crook too."

"Well you can have some lunch now and a proper meal tonight, but you're out in the morning," she'd reply, matter-of-factly.

"Orright, Missus Sayer, thanks," Dan would say politely. "Can you give Digger a feed too, please?"

It was mostly observing Dipso Dan that led me to believe there's a patron saint of drunks. He was indestructible. I've seen him fall down on the concrete outside the cafe and not even drop his shopping. I've seen him fall over the pub verandah at the Royal without breaking the two bottles of beer he had wrapped in brown paper. He would stagger erect in one jerky movement and continue on his wobbly pilgrimage as if nothing had happened.

The other amazing thing was that you could never get the better of him. I remember Dougie calling the sergeant to remove him from the Tatts one night when he'd been particularly obnoxious. Big Bill Sayer appeared within minutes and, filling the door of the pub in his police uniform, said, "C'mon Dan, you're coming with me. You drink too much!"

Dipso didn't miss a beat, "Don't be s ...silly, sergeant," he slurred, swaying on the spot, "you can't!"

My favourite Dipso Dan story concerns the time he supposedly backed a winner with the SP bookie and made a real nuisance of himself until Doug threw him out of the Tatts. Eddy Pierce's cab was parked outside and Dipso jumped straight in. With his mind totally befuddled by booze he told Eddy he wanted to go to the Tatts for a drink.

"We're at the Tatts now," replied Eddy.

"Strecoth, so we are!" yelled Dipso, fumbling in his pocket and staggering out of the cab. "Here's your money and you shouldn't drive so bloody fast!"

As I wasn't there when that happened, I can only assume it's true. I've seen Dipso do some pretty funny things. I can see him now, in my mind's eye — weaving and bouncing jerkily along the main street of Weelabarabak, talking non-stop to Digger as he goes. And the more I think about him and that crazy dancing motion of his, the more convinced I am that there's a patron saint of drunks. Perhaps it's St Vitus.

# The Rankine Store [from *Packhorse Drover*]
## Bruce Simpson

The Rankine store, complete with bottle licence, was on the Rankine (or Ranken) River about 40 miles (65 kilometres) from the Alexandra homestead. It was always spelled "Rankine" by the drovers and the owners of the store but usually appears as "Ranken" on modern maps. As it was situated on country mustered by the stock camp, the store proved over the years to be a headache to managers of the sprawling cattle property. Finally, bowing to the inevitable, they gave tacit approval to the ringers to have a few days off whenever they mustered past the place.

One hears a lot about endurance riders these days. Once, for a bet, Cammy Cleary rode a horse from Alexandria to the Rankine and back, a round trip of 80 miles (130 kilometres) between sun-up and sundown. He took a bottle of Fowler's rum back as proof. Not bad for a grass-fed stockhorse.

In my time Jim Fowler and his good wife catered to the needs of the drovers and ringers. Jimmy had been head stockman on Alexandria and was a top rough rider who once rode a grey outlaw call The Snake. He was a bit of a showman, handy with his fists and a real artist with a whip. I once saw a big young ringer challenge Jimmy to hop outside then put his fists up. After a moment's thought Jimmy agreed, but on his way outside he made a detour through the kitchen, where he emptied one of his wife's pepper pots into his left fist. The bout was a brief one: Jimmy threw a straight left, opening his fist at the end of the punch; the right cross that followed flattened his half-blinded opponent.

Wason Byers, one of the Territory's rougher denizens, dropped into the Rankine one day when we were all there. He was after a couple of chaps, he told us, who he claimed had maligned him. He caught up with them in Mrs Fowler's kitchen, where a leg of goat was roasting for dinner. Wason dropped one of the alleged offenders then, grabbing the other, he sat the struggling ringer on the hot stove top and held him there. For a while it looked as though the night's menu of roast goat would be augmented by roast ringer.

One day at the Rankine Reg Winton and I got into a debate on rushes. He contended any animals would rush, while I believed highly domesticated ones would not, despite the opinion of a drunken cook who kept relating how he had seen thirty cats rush and take the side out of a meat house at McArthur River. The debate was an amicable one and I forgot about it until on the way back to the camp, Reg stopped beside Mrs Fowler's goat yard. Mrs Fowler had over a hundred goats that provided meat and milk for the isolated settlement. They were penned every night in a large yard that had an iron-roofed shed in one corner for shelter.

"Now," said Reg, "let's settle this rush business."

He climbed up the fence and then carefully made his way on to the roof of the shed. The goats camped around the yard took no notice of the intruder, until he suddenly leapt in the air, landing with a bellow in the middle of the iron roof. The result was instantaneous and devastating: the goats flattened one side of the compound and disappeared at high speed into the night. Reg made his point, but our reception at the store next day was decidedly frosty.

During those times when we were at the Rankine, we always camped at the one-mile waterhole in the river just below the store. It was an easy walk sober, but for those of us who overdid it at Fowlers' it became something between a marathon and an army obstacle course. At one time we had in the camp a cook who had made a fortune at Tennant Creek. He had blown it all in Sydney, with the exception of a top dental plate specially made for him from gold from his mine. One morning we awoke to find our cook missing. He later staggered into camp, a hungover and heartbroken wreck, crying that he'd lost his fangs. He had apparently got lost and wandered around in circles most of the night. He had had a number of big spits during his drunken wanderings and no doubt his teeth had taken flight on one of these occasions.

After some merriment at the cook's expense, we poured a rum into him and all hands set out to track down the lost dentures. I could not help thinking of Jason and his search for the Golden Fleece, only this time it was the search for the Golden Teeth. Finally one of the group found the cook's last link with his affluent past. The relieved owner picked up his dentures and, after wiping them briefly on his trousers, popped them into his mouth and headed up to the store for another rum.

"If you were only to peep into the Sydney police office on a Monday forenoon, you would then see a lovely specimen of our morality. Scores of men, women, boys and girls, who had been dragged off the streets on the preceding evening for drunkenness standing with brazen faces to hear their respective sentences."

THE REV. DAVID MCKENZIE, 1845

# The Rising of the Court
## Henry Lawson

*Oh, then tell us, Kings and Judges, where our meeting is to be,*
*When the laws of men are nothing and our spirits all are free —*
*When the laws of men are nothing, and no wealth can hold the fort,*
*There'll be thirst for mighty brewers at the Rising of the Court.*

The same dingy courtroom, deep and dim, like a well, with the clock high up on the wall, and the doors low down in it; with the bench, which, with some gilding, might be likened to a gingerbread imitation of a throne; the royal arms above it and the little witness box to one side, where so many honest people are bullied, insulted and laughed at by third-rate blackguardly little "lawyers", and so many pitiful, pathetic and noble lies are told by pitiful sinners and disreputable heroes for a little liberty for a lost self, or for the sake of a friend, of a "pal" or a "cobber". The same overworked and underpaid magistrate trying to keep his attention fixed on the same old miserable scene before him, as a weary, overworked and underpaid journalist or author strives to keep his attention fixed on his proofs. The same row of big, strong, healthy, good-natured policemen trying not to grin at times; and the police court solicitors ("The place stinks with 'em," a sergeant told me) wrangling over some miserable case for a crust, and the "reporters", shabby some of them, eager to get a brutal joke for their papers out of the accumulated mass of misery before them, whether it be at the expense of the deaf, blind, or crippled man, or the alien.

And opposite the bench the dock, divided by a partition, with the women to the left and the men to the right. But, over there, on a form to one side of the bench, opposite the witness box and as the one bright spot in this dark and shameful and useless scene, and in a patch of sunlight from the skylight as it happens, sit representatives of the Prisoners' Aid Society, Prison Gate and Rescue Brigades, etc. (one or two of the ladies in nurses' uniforms), who are come to help us and to fight for us against the Law of their Land and of ours, God help us!

Mrs Johnson, of Red Rock Lane, is here, and her rival in revolution, One-Eyed Kate, and Cock-Eyed Sal, and one or two of the other aristocrats of the alley. And the weeping bedraggled remains of what was once, and not so long ago, a pretty, slight, fair-haired and blue-eyed Australian girl. She is up for inciting One-Eyed Kate to resist the police. Also, Three-Pea Ginger, Stousher, and Wingy, for some participation in the row amongst the aforementioned ladies. (Wingy, by the way, is a ratty little one-armed man, whose case is usually described in the headline, as "A 'Armless Case", by one of our great dailies.) And their pals are waiting outside in the vestibule, Frowsy Kate (The Red Streak), Boko Bill, Pincher and his "piece", etc., getting together the stuff for the possible fines, and the ten bob fee for the lawyer, in one case, and ready to swear to anything if called upon. And I myself, though I have not yet entered Red Rock Lane Society, on bail, on a charge of "plain drunk". It was "drunk and disorderly" by the way, but a kindly sergeant changed it to plain drunk (though I always thought my drunk was ornamental).

Yet I am not ashamed — only comfortably dulled and a little tired; dully interested and observant, hopeful for the sunlight presently. We low persons get too great a contempt for things to feel much ashamed at any time; and this very contempt keeps many of us from "reforming". We hear too many lies sworn that we *know* to be lies, and see too many unjust and brutal things done that we know to be brutal and unjust.

But let us go back a bit, and suppose we are still waiting for the magistrate, and think of Last Night. "Silence!" But from no human voice this time. The whispering, shuffling, and clicking of the court typewriter ceases, the scene darkens, and the court is blotted out as a scene is blotted out from the sight of a man who has thrown himself into a mesmeric trance. And:

Drink, lurid recollection of being "searched", clang of iron cell door, and I grope for and crawl onto the slanting plank. Period of oblivion, or the soul is away in some other world. Clang of cell door again, and soul returns in a hurry to take heed of another soul, belonging to a belated drunk on the plank by my side. Other soul says: "Gotta match?"

So we're not in Hell yet.

We fumble and light up. They leave us our pipes, tobacco and matches; presently, one knocks with his pipe on the iron trap of the door and asks for water, which is brought in a tin pint pot. Then follow intervals of smoking, incoherent mutterings that pass for conversation, borrowings of matches, knocking with the pannikin on the cell door wicket or trap for more water, matches, and bail; false and fitful starts into slumber, perhaps, or wild attempts at flight on the part of our souls into that other world that the sober and sane know nothing of; and, gradually, suddenly it seems, reason (if this world is reasonable) comes back.

"What's your trouble?"

"Don't know. Bomb outrage, perhaps."

"Drunk?"

"Yes."

"What's yours?"

"Same boat."

But presently he is plainly uneasy (and I am getting that way, too, to tell the truth), and, after moving about, and walking up and down in the narrow space as well as we can, he "rings up" another policeman, who happens to be the fat one who is to be in charge all night.

"Wot's up here?"

"What have I been up to?"

"Killin' a Chinaman. Go to sleep."

Policeman peers in at me inquiringly, but I forbear to ask questions.

Blankets are thrown in by a friend of mine in the force, though we are not entitled to them until we are bailed or removed to the "paddock" (the big drunks' dormitory and dining cell at the Central), and we proceed to make ourselves comfortable. My mate wonders whether he asked them to send to his wife to get bail, and hopes he didn't.

They have left our wicket open, seeing, or rather hearing, that we are quiet. But they have seemingly left some other wickets open also, for from a neighbouring cell comes the voice of Mrs Johnson holding forth. The locomotive has apparently just been run into the cleaning sheds and her fires have not had time to cool. They say that Mrs Johnson was a "lady once", like many of her kind; that she is not a "bad woman", that is, not a woman of loose character, but gets money sent to her from somewhere, from her "family", or her husband perhaps. But when she lets herself loose, or, rather, when the beer lets her loose, she is a tornado and a terror in Red Rock Lane, and it is only her fierce, practical kindness to her unfortunate or poverty-stricken sisters in her sober moments that keeps her forgiven in that classic thoroughfare. She can certainly speak "like a lady" when she likes, and like an intelligent, even a clever, woman — not like a "woman of the world", but as a woman who knew and knows the world, and is in hell. But now her language is the language of a rough shearer in a "rough shed" on a blazing hot day.

After a while my mate calls out to her: "Oh! For God's sake give it a rest!"

Whereupon Mrs Johnson straightway opens on him and his ancestry, and his mental, moral, and physical condition — especially the latter. She accuses him of every crime known to Christian countries and some Asiatic and ancient ones. She wants to know how long he has been out of jail for kicking his wife to pieces that time when she was up as a witness against him, and whether he is in for the same thing again. (She has never set eyes on him, by the way, nor he on her.)

He calls back that she is not a respectable woman, and he knows all about her.

Thereupon she shrieks at him and bangs and kicks at her door, and demands his name and address. It would appear that she is a respectable woman, and hundreds can prove it, and she is going to make him prove it in open court.

He calls back that his name is Percy Reginald Grainger, and his town residence is "The Mansions", Macleay Street, next to Mr Isaacs, the magistrate, and he also gives her the address of his solicitor.

She bangs and shrieks again, and states that she will get his name from the charge sheet in the morning and have him up for criminal libel, and have his cell mate up as a witness, and hers, too. But just here a policeman comes along and closes her wicket with a bang and cuts her off, so that her statements become indistinct, or come only as shrieks from a lost soul in an underground dungeon. He also threatens to cut us off and smother us if we don't shut up. I wonder whether they've got her in the padded cell.

Sleep for a while. I wonder whether they'll give us time, or we'll be able to sleep some of our sins off in the end, as we sleep our drink off here? Then "The Paddock" and daylight; but there's little time for the Paddock here, for we must soon be back in court. The men borrow and lend and divide tobacco, lend even pipes, while some break up hard tobacco and roll cigarettes with bits of newspaper. If it is Sunday morning, even those who have no hope for bail and have a long horrible day and night before them will sometimes join in a cheer as the more fortunate are bailed. But the others have tea and bread and butter brought to them by one of the Prisoners' Aid societies, who ask for no religion in return. They come to save bodies, and not to fish for souls. The men walk up and down and to and fro, and cross and recross incessantly, as caged men and animals always do, and as some uncaged men do, too.

"Any of you gentlemen want breakfast?" Those who have money and appetites order; some order for the sake of the tea alone, and some "shout" two or three extra breakfasts for those who had nothing on them when they were run in. We low people can be very kind to each other in trouble. But now it's time to call us out by the lists, marshal us up in the passage and draft us into court. Ladies first. But I forgot that I am out on bail, and that the foregoing belongs to another occasion. Or was it only imagination, or hearsay? Journalists have got themselves run in before now, in order to see and hear and feel and smell for themselves, and write.

"Silence! Order in the court." I come like a shot out of my nightmare or trance, or what you will, and we all rise as the magistrate takes his seat. None of us noticed him come in, but he's there, and I've a quaint idea that he bowed to his audience. Kindly, humorous Mr Isaacs, whom we have lost, always gave me that idea. And, while he looks over his papers the women seem to group themselves, unconsciously as it were, with Mrs Johnson in front centre, as though they depended on her in some vague way. She has slept it off and tidied, or been tidied, up, and is as clear-headed as she ever will be. Crouching directly behind her, supported and comforted on one side by One-Eyed Kate, and on the other by Cock-Eyed Sal, is the poor bedraggled little resister of the law, sobbing convulsively, her breasts and thin shoulders heaving and shaking under her open-work blouse. There's very little inciting to resist about her now. Most women can cry when they like, I know, and many have cried men to gaol and the gallows; but here in this place, if a woman's tears can avail her anything, who, save perhaps a police court solicitor and gentleman-by-Act-of-Parliament would, or dare, raise a sneer?

His Worship looks up.

Mrs Johnson (from the dock): "Good morning, Mr Isaacs. How do you do? You're looking very well this morning, Mr Isaacs."

His Worship (from the Bench): "Thank you, Mrs Johnson. I'm feeling very well this morning."

There's a pause, but there is no "laughter". The would-be satellites don't know whom the laugh might be against. His Worship bends over the papers again, and I can see that he is having trouble with that quaintly humorous and kindly smile, or grin, of his. He has a hard job to control his smile and get it off his face as some magistrates have to get a smile onto theirs. And there's a case coming by-and-by that he'll have to look a bit serious over. However —

"Jane Johnson!"

Mrs Johnson is here present, and reminds the Sergeant that she is.

Then begins, or does begin in most courts, the same dreary old drone, like the giving out of a hymn, of the same dreary old charge: "You — Are — Charged — With — Being — Drunk — And — Disorderly — In — Such — And — Such — A — Street — How — Do — You — Plead — Guilty — Or — Not — Guilty?" But they are less orthodox here. The "disorderly" has dropped out of Mrs Johnson's charge somehow, on the way from the charge room. I don't know what has been going on behind the scenes, but it is Christmas time and the sergeant seems anxious to let Mrs Johnson off lightly. It means anything from twenty-four hours or five shillings to three months on the Island for her. The lawyers and the police, especially the lawyers, are secretly afraid of Mrs Johnson.

The Sergeant: "This woman has not been here for six weeks, your Worship."

Mrs Johnson (who has him set and has been waiting for him for a year or so): "It's a damned lie, Mr Isaacs. I was here last Wednesday!" Then, after a horrified pause in the Court: "But I beg *your* pardon, Mr Isaacs."

His Worship's head goes down again. The "laughter" doesn't come here, either. There is a whispered consultation, and (it being Christmas time) they compromise with Mrs Johnson for "five shillings or the rising" and she thanks his Worship and is escorted out, rather more hurriedly than is comfortable with her dignity, for she makes remarks about it.

The members of the Johnsonian sisterhood have reason to be thankful for the "lift" she has given them, for they all get off lightly, and even the awful resister of Law-an'-order is forgiven.

Next time poor Mrs Johnson will leave *en route* for "Th' Island" and stay there three months.

The sisters join Mrs Johnson, who has some money and takes them to a favourite haunt and shouts for them, as she does for the boys sometimes. Their opinions on civilisation are not to be printed.

Ginger and Wingy get off with the option, and, though the fine is heavy, it is paid. They adjourn with Boko Bill and their politics are lurid.

Squinny Peters (plain drunk, five bob or the risin'), who is peculiar for always paying his fine, elects to take it out this time. It appears that the last time Squinny got five bob or the risin' he ante'd up the splosh like a man, and the court rose immediately, to Squinny's intense disgust. He isn't taking any chances this time.

Wild-Flowers-Charley, who recently did a fortnight, and has been out on bail, has had a few this morning, and, in spite of warnings from and promises to friends, insists on making a statement, though by simply pleading guilty he might get off easily.

The statement lasts some ten minutes. Mr Isaacs listens patiently and politely and remarks:

"Fourteen days."

Charley saw the humour of it afterwards, he says.

But what good does it all do?

I had no wish to treat drunkenness frivolously in beginning this sketch; I have seen women in the horrors — that ought to be enough.

> "Be not drunk with wine, wherein is excess; but be filled with the Spirit."
>
> EPHESIANS 5:18

# The Mixture
# As Never Before
## Lennie Lower

A festive air seems to be pervading the district. The peasantry are warming up in preparation for the usual bout of Christmas and New Year parties. Your poor Uncle Lennie is just getting over a cocktail party, and there is another one looming on the horizon.

I never did care much for cocktail parties. I'm all the time looking for a place to put the olive stones. You can't park them under the table like chewing gum. Cherries are easy; they just go down whole with the drink, toothpick and all.

Just recently I flung a party for Arbuthnot, my grandfather, in celebration of his reaching the age of discretion. Having reached the age of ninety-five, he found that his financial resources were so limited that discretion looked the best shot on the table.

I made the cocktails in the washtubs, and we had a few cases of whisky for the teetotallers. Ever tasted an Angel's Smack? I can mix an Angel's Smack, a Horse's Neck, a Sidecar or a Viper's Breath just like mother used to make. Good stuff, too. You can get happy washing up the glasses.

I had a lot of trouble with the savouries, or horse devours as the French call them. The average hostess's idea of a savoury is to butter a biscuit and plonk a bean on top of it. Some, I'll admit, make such an artistic mess of gherkins, anchovies, chillies and cheese that the whole biscuit is suitable for framing, and only a vandal would eat it. But I invented a savoury composed of a hard-boiled egg and sandsoap. All the guests said it was a wow.

My grandfather came forward with a suggestion for a biscuit soaked in bromide with an aspirin tablet embedded in it. This was one of the few sensible suggestions he made during my preparations for the party.

Have you ever paused in your mad rush to the sideboard and considered what a lot of work has gone into the making of those cocktails and savouries you're wolfing down like a famished greyhound? I spent hours at those washtubs, pouring in this and that: a bit of gin, a dash of bitters, a bucket of absinthe, a handful of curry, my wristwatch (this was unintentional, but I may tell you that after I had fished it out it has been gaining an hour every five minutes, and when I go to put it on it walks away from me) and some stale beer and boot polish and vermouth, French vermouth and Italian vermouth. I wasn't game to put in any Abyssinian vermouth. Anyhow, seeing that both the French and the Italian vermouths were made in Australia, it didn't matter much.

Then I had to boil a copper full of frankfurters, and I had to open tin after tin of *petit poisson* (French, means sardines). Tasted like poisson, too, after I'd finished with them.

When the guests arrived they all hung about like people do at cocktail parties, talking about racehorses and books and pictures and what a rotten hat Mrs. Stogers had on, and how Miss Flethers, who was always talking about quarrels with her dressmaker, usually got her frocks at the jumble sale in aid of the Sunday school picnic … you know.

Then when the gun went they fell upon my savouries and I was kept busy dashing backwards and forwards to the washtubs and ladling out cocktails. Fortunately I ran short of olives and had to use nutmegs, which seemed to slow them up a bit. There are no stones in nutmegs, by the way. Just thought I'd tell you.

Then Arbuthnot made a speech. We tried to stop him but he threatened to pull the plugs out of the washtubs, so we let him go.

"Ladies and gentlemen," he said. "I wish to thank you all for coming here and burning holes in the furniture and eating us out of house and home. As you all know, I have now reached the age of discretion, when I have to live on charcoal biscuits and sterilised dill water. It has taken me years and years to reach this happy state and, believe me, the happiest times of my life were spent in acquiring my present nervous debility, gout, dyspepsia and various duodenal ulcers."

The guests then pulled him off the piano and locked him in the bathroom. Following which, one of my guests asked me what the devil I was doing hanging about the place, and why wasn't there any music or something, and I got thrown back into the wash-house and told to make more cocktails.

So I put four gallons of prussic acid in the mixture and served it out. They all said it was great and asked for more. That's what cocktail drinking does to your system. Either you succumb after the first few weeks, or you become immune and unpoisonable.

Any of you girls who have a secret yearning for the bright lights had better be warned against cocktail parties. Many an innocent girl has learned to chew gum at a cocktail party, to the utter horror of her parents, who have hurled her out into the snow to battle through life alone and unaided without a soul to care whether she lived or died, and finished up in a squalid tenement scantily clad in filthy rags and dying neglected, with a bag of cocaine clutched in her hand.

There, there, now! I've made you cry! Uncle didn't mean it as bad as that. He just wants you to be warned, that's all. If any dark and handsome stranger approaches you and offers you a cocktail, spurn him. Stick to rum.

> "The worst thing about some men is that when they are not drunk they are sober."
>
> WILLIAM BUTLER YEATS, 1921

# Nelly
## "Ah Chee" (The *Bulletin* 1889)

She was very pretty. All Nellies are. She had silky-brown hair with a charming ripple in it; beautiful hazel eyes, and long, delicate ears. She was a retriever. And she belonged to Penn.

Penn, nobody knew him by any other name, was immeasurably the inferior animal, being a drunken old Cornishman. He was a "hatter", partly by choice, for his disposition was surly and solitary, and partly because no mate had ever been able to put up with his ingrained crabbedness.

"Seems to me that Old Penn's the sourest old bugger on the field," said Jimmy Squareface of the Miner's Arms. "Drunk or sober, it don't make no difference to *him*. And nobody ever seed him shout, no matter how tight he got. My 'pinion of old Penn is, he's no blanky good!"

And this opinion was held and expressed, more or less profanely, by everyone except Nelly on Mick's diggings.

And Nelly? To her, Penn was the embodiment of all that was noble, and grand, and estimable in mankind. She loved the very clay-stained moleskins he wore, and even their supporting belt, which the old sinner only took off to "leather" her with. And the more he leathered her, the more she clung to him and fawned on him, and snapped at all who came near him, when Nelly's superior wisdom told her that her master had too much whisky aboard to be able to look after himself.

Nelly was otherwise useful to her master. Penn did not keep a housemaid and Nelly, recognising this deficiency in the domestic economy, supplied the want to the best of her ability. When Penn finished a meal he set his plate and pannikin on the floor before Nelly, and she polished them as brightly as could any scullery maid in the country. Then Penn, who knew or cared nothing about hydatid cysts, put his dishes away in the gin-case which served him for a table and all was ready for the next meal.

But the greatest service that Nelly rendered Penn was the care she took of him when he went on one of his periodical sprees. I think she used to be rather surprised that the object of her affections should become so helpless and stupid, but she only increased her attentions, and tended him with truly feminine care. She would try every possible plan to induce him to come home, and when these had all proved futile she would guard him from the approach of all comers with the most determined vigilance. Penn was a hardy old villain, and always stubbornly refused to sleep at the pub. Whatever the weather, he would go to the big gum tree outside the yard and beneath it, on the bare ground, he would camp. In the morning he would awake, curse, brush the frost from his beard, kick Nelly and resume his spree with a moroseness that seemed inseparable from him and with a total absence of enthusiasm. This would last as long as Penn's money did. When that was all gone, and the publican chillingly refused to "chalk it" to any extent, Penn sobered up.

"I'm goin' home," said Penn to the landlord. "Give us a bottle." His hand shook, his face was flushed, he muttered uneasily to himself at times and cast a frightened look around. Plainly, he was developing a most interesting case of DTs. He got the bottle, and started for home.

Nelly's joy was extravagant. She very nearly overturned the old man as she leaped upon him to show her satisfaction. But all she got in return was a smite from Penn's fist, as he yelled: "Curse you, get out! You've got blood on you!"

This was untrue. But a suspicion that all was not right with Nelly had arisen in Penn's mind, and he was unable to allay it. And the more he looked at Nelly (she kept at a discreet distance now) the more abnormal her appearance seemed. "Where did she get them two heads of hers?" her master wondered vaguely. But the two heads were driven quite out of his thoughts by the big crawfish that were fighting on Nelly's back, and the death adders that were tying themselves in knots round her neck and making faces at him all the while. Then what multitudes of strange birds were flying around her! She must be dead, surely, or all those big yellow crows would not be there! He would throw a stone at her and hunt her away. But when he stooped for a stone the grass was so full of frogs with sharp, cruel beaks that he daren't put his hand down. He would throw that big rock he had in his pocket, and which had been such a burden to him so long. How did it come there, anyhow? With shaking hand he took out the bottle of rum and threw it feebly at the dog. But she only grinned the more, and the snakes round her neck untwined themselves and came after him. He would run. He wasn't goin' to be bitten by no death-adders, not he! But he stubbed his toe against a stump and hit the ground with his head, and slept.

When he awoke it was bright moonlight. There were not so many snakes about; but his head was very bad and would not stay with him, except for a few seconds. And too think all this misery was owing to that sanguinary dog! He would put her out for it, *that* he would!

He pulled himself together, and walked home, Nelly showing the way inside the hut. She had got rid of the crawfish and the snakes, Penn noted. But who could tell when they would come again and frighten him? She must be put out of the way, "for good".

Penn took the saddle-strap that served him from his waist. "Here, Nelly!" he said.

Nelly came up gladly. Penn lifted her two forepaws, crossed them on the back of her neck, and fastened them there with the strap. Then he lifted her up, and went out towards the creek.

Trustful old Nelly! She didn't even whine, so sure was she that one she loved so much could not harm her. And if she lost her faith as she went under, she never came to the top to say so.

Penn recovered, of course, in a few days. He always did. But he was too hardened an old ruffian to be sorry for what he had done; and, indeed, he remembered it but dimly. But since then his crockery has never been cleaned. That is no great hardship for Penn, however. He is not fastidious.

# McCarthy's Brew
## George Essex Evans

The team of Black McCarthy crawled adown the Norman road,
The ground was bare, the bullocks spare, and grievous was the load,
The brown hawks wheeled above them and the heatwaves throbbed and
    glowed.

With lolling tongues and bloodshot eyes and sinews all astrain,
McCarthy's bullocks staggered on across the sun-cracked plain,
The waggon lumbered after with the drivers raising Cain.

Three mournful figures sat around the campfire's fitful glare,
McKinlay Jim and "Spotty" and McCarthy's self were there,
But their spirits were so dismal that they couldn't raise a swear!

'Twas not the long, dry stage ahead that made those bold hearts shrink,
The drought-cursed ground, the dying stock, the water thick as ink,
But, the drinking curse was on them and they had no grog to drink!

Then with a bound up from the ground McCarthy jumped and cried:
"'Tis vain! 'Tis vain! I go insane. These pangs in my inside!
Some sort of grog, for love of God, invent, concoct, provide!"

McKinlay Jim straight answered him: "Those lotions, sauce and things
Should surely make a brew to slake these thirstful sufferings,
A brew that slakes, a brew that wakes and burns and bucks and stings."

Down came the cases from the load — they wrenched them wide with
    force.
They poured and mixed and stirred a brew that would have killed
    a horse,
Cayenne, painkiller, pickles, embrocation, Worcester sauce!

Oh wild and high and fierce and free the orgy rose that night;
The songs they sang, the deeds they did, no poet could indite;
To see them pass that billy round, it was a fearsome sight.

The dingo heard them and with tail between his legs he fled!
The curlew saw them and he ceased his wailing for the dead!
Each frightened bullock on the plain went straightway off his head!

Alas! and there are those who say that at the dawn of day
Three perforated carriers round a smouldering campfire lay:
They did not think McCarthy's brew would take them in that way!

McCarthy's teams at Normanton no more the Gulf men see.
McCarthy's bullocks roam the wilds exuberant and free;
McCarthy lies, an instance of preserved anatomee!

Go, take the moral of this rhyme, which in deep grief I write:
Don't ever drink McCarthy's brew. Be warned in case you might —
Gulf whisky kills at twenty yards, but this stuff kills at sight!

> "Australians have always been enthusiasitic if not particularly intelligent drinkers."
>
> SIDNEY J. BAKER, 1945

# Anzac Night in The Gardens
## Lennie Lower

Lost in the wilds of the Botanic Gardens! Heavens, shall we ever forget it! The last human face we saw was that of Matthew Flinders, the great explorer.

We got in with a few Anzacs last night, and we forget how we got into the Gardens, but believe us, it's terrible. Instructive, but terrible.

Nothing to drink but goldfish.

Bottle-trees dotted about the place, and we had no opener. Naked men and women standing on square whitewashed rocks. All dumb!

We wandered up to a signboard, thinking to read, "Ten miles to …," and saw there, "Please do not walk on the grass borders."

Starving, practically, we climbed a coconut tree for food and found it was a date tree without any dates on it.

We came to a tree marked "Dysoxolum". We thought, we *knew*, how sox were dyed, but what shall it profit a man if he lose himself in the Gardens?

We came to where the tortoise slept, and knocked on his shell. Like all the rest of our friends, he was in, but he didn't answer.

Dawn found us clawing at the front of the Herbarium, shrieking hysterically for just a little thyme.

The keeper who found us said that everything was all right and this was the way out. We don't know what became of the others.

Probably their bodies will be found in the bandstand and identified by their pawn tickets.

The Anzacs certainly were, and still are, a tough crowd.

We will never go into the Gardens again without wearing all our medals and two identification discs.

It's always best to carry a spare on Anzac night.

> "There aren't many countries in the world where people get the DTs on beer. Australia is one of them."
>
> DR E. CUNNINGHAM-DAX, 1969

# Rats
## Henry Lawson

"Why, there's two of them, and they're having a fight! Come on."

It seemed a strange place for a fight, that hot, lonely cottonbush plain. And yet not more than half a mile ahead there were apparently two men struggling together on the track.

The three travellers postponed their smoke-oh and hurried on. They were shearers — a little man and a big man, known respectively as "Sunlight" and "Macquarie", and a tall, thin, young jackaroo whom they called "Milky".

"I wonder where the other man sprang from? I didn't see him before," said Sunlight.

"He muster bin layin' down in the bushes," said Macquarie. "They're goin' at it proper, too. Come on! Hurry up and see the fun!"

They hurried on.

"It's a funny-lookin' feller, the other feller," panted Milky. "He don't seem to have no head. Look! He's down, they're both down! They must ha' clinched on the ground. No! they're up an' at it again ... Why, good Lord! I think the other's a woman!"

"My oath! So it is!" yelled Sunlight. "Look! The brute's got her down again! He's kickin' her! Come on, chaps; come on, or he'll do for her!"

They dropped swags, waterbags and all, and raced forward; but presently Sunlight, who had the best eyes, slackened his pace and dropped behind. His mates glanced back at his face, saw a peculiar expression there, looked ahead again, and then dropped into a walk.

They reached the scene of the trouble and there stood a little withered old man by the track, with his arms folded close up under his chin; he was dressed mostly in calico patches and half a dozen corks, suspended on bits of string from the brim of his hat, dangled before his bleared optics to scare away the flies. He was scowling malignantly at a stout, dumpy swag which lay in the middle of the track.

"Well, old Rats, what's the trouble?" asked Sunlight.

"Oh, nothing, nothing," answered the old man, without looking round. "I fell out with my swag, that's all. He knocked me down, but I've settled him."

"But look here," said Sunlight, winking at his mates, "we saw you jump on him when he was down. That ain't fair, you know."

"But you didn't see it all," cried Rats, getting excited. "He hit *me* down first! And, look here, I'll fight him again for nothing, and you can see fair play."

They talked a while, then Sunlight proposed to second the swag, while his mate supported the old man, and after some persuasion Milky agreed, for the sake of the lark, to act as timekeeper and referee.

Rats entered into the spirit of the thing; he stripped to the waist, and while he was getting ready the travellers pretended to bet on the result.

Macquarie took his place behind the old man, and Sunlight upended the swag. Rats shaped and danced round; then he rushed, feinted, ducked, retreated, darted in once more and suddenly went down like a shot on the broad of his back. No actor could have done it better; he went down from that imaginary blow as if a cannonball had struck him in the forehead.

Milky called time, and the old man came up, looking shaky. However, he got in a tremendous blow which knocked the swag into the bushes.

Several rounds followed with varying success.

The men pretended to get more and more excited and betted freely, and Rats did his best. At last they got tired of the fun, Sunlight let the swag lie after Milky called time, and the jackaroo awarded the fight to Rats. They pretended to hand over the stakes, and then went back for their swags, while the old man put on his shirt.

Then he calmed down, carried his swag to the side of the track, sat down on it and talked rationally about bush matters for a while; but presently he grew silent and began to feel his muscles and smile idiotically.

"Can you len' us a bit o' meat?" said he suddenly.

They spared him half a pound; but he said he didn't want it all, and cut off about an ounce, which he laid on the end of his swag. Then he took the lid off his billy and produced a fishing-line. He baited the hook, threw the line across the track and waited for a bite. Soon he got deeply interested in the line, jerked it once or twice, and drew it in rapidly. The bait had been rubbed off in the grass. The old man regarded the hook disgustedly.

"Look at that!" he cried. "I had him, only I was in such a hurry. I should ha' played him a little more."

Next time he was more careful; he drew the line in warily, grabbed an imaginary fish and laid it down on the grass. Sunlight and Co were greatly interested by this time.

"Wot yer think o' that?" asked Rats. "It weighs thirty pound if it weighs an ounce! Wot yer think o' that for a cod? The hook's half way down his blessed gullet."

He caught several cod and bream while they were there, and invited them to camp and have tea with him. But they wished to reach a certain shed next day, so, after the ancient had borrowed about a pound of meat for bait, they went on, and left him fishing contentedly.

But first Sunlight went down into his pocket and came up with half a crown, which he gave to the old man, along with some tucker. "You'd best push on to the water before dark, old chap," he said, kindly.

When they turned their heads again Rats was still fishing: but when they looked back for the last time before entering the timber, he was having another row with his swag; and Sunlight reckoned that the trouble arose out of some lies the swag had been telling about the bigger fish it caught.

> **"Sometimes too much drink is barely enough."**
>
> MARK TWAIN, 1902

## from ... Doogan
### C.J. Dennis

Doogan's a byword, Doogan's a butt, Doogan's the town disgrace:
Loafin' around in his dirty clo'es, down at the heel an' out at the
    toes,
Cadgin' a drink from the fellers he knows, workin' from place to
    place.
Beggin' for work when he's down-an'-out, toilin' a while an' then:
Doogan, Doogan, Dithery Doogan, lickerin' up again.

Doogan was once the township's pride; youthful, wealthy an' wild,
Free an' easy and devil-may-care, into the thick of it everywhere;
With a house an' land and a spankin' pair, an' a beautiful wife
    an' child.
Welcome he was as the flowers in May an' a popular man with
    men;
Doogan, Doogan, Dashaway Doogan, racketin' round again.

Champagne suppers it was them days, horses an' dogs an' sport.
Dashaway Doogan led the dance; Daredevil Doogan took the
    chance,
An' none was there with a warnin' glance, but all to flatter an'
    court.
For Dashaway Doogan called the tune, an' who was to pay the
    score.
But Doogan, Doogan, Dashaway Doogan, fillin' 'em up once more.

*He spent his money, he lost his land, he buried his wife an' child*
*All in the space of a year they say, then Dashaway Doogan*
*    drifted away*
*With never a sign for many a day, but many's the tale an' wild*
*They told of his doin's when I was a girl, told with a laugh an'*
*    a sigh,*
*Of Dashaway Doogan, Drinkin' Doogan, king of the days*
*    gone by.*

*He came back here when his hair was grey, pinnin' his hopes to*
*    the town,*
*And hung out a sign as an auctioneer, then agent, wheat buyer, all*
*    in a year.*
*But none could trust him, because of the beer: an' how could he*
*    go, but down?*
*Early an' late he was over the way, thick with the drinkin' men*
*Doogan, Doogan, Dissolute Doogan, fillin' 'em up again.*

*Down the ladder he quickly ran, an' how could he hope but fail?*
*He drank till he hadn't a coin to spend; he drank till he hadn't a*
*    worthy friend;*
*He drank till he stole, an' that was the end, an' a couple of*
*    months in jail …*
*Now he's the soak an' the odd-job-man, loafer, rouseabout, clown:*
*Doogan, Doogan, Dilly ole Doogan, lowest in all the town.*

*I often wonder what Doogan thinks as he shuffles along out there,*
*Off on his errand of cadgin' beers, passin' his friends of the early*
*    years,*
*An' some of 'em pities an' some of 'em sneers. But Doogan? Oh he*
*    don't care.*
*He calls 'em all by their Christian names, George an' Harry an'*
*    Ben:*
*Doogan, Doogan, Draggety Doogan, cadgin' around again.*

*Doogan failin' in these last years, an' he'll end as all of 'em do,*
*The fine free fellers who never can save, the devil-may-cares who*
*    won't behave,*
*An' they'll rattle him off to a pauper's grave, an' a real good*
*    riddance too.*
*With never a sigh for his passin' by, an' never a friend to weep*
*When Dashaway Doogan, Dithery Doogan, goes to his sober*
*    sleep.*

# The Enlightenment

# Introduction

Here are diverse accounts of the realisations, the conclusions drawn, the fallout and the final understandings of the consequences of drinking. In all of these stories there is a point where some sort of light dawns, either for the story-teller or for some among the participants or observers, perhaps even for those in the audience, dear reader.

Some of these stories are accounts of self-realisation. In this category some, like "Miners' Holiday", are poignant well-crafted stories of lost possibilities; some, like "Over the Wine", are almost maudlin nostalgic accounts of thwarted ambition; others, like "A Bush Publican's Lament", are rough-and-ready tongue-in-cheek satire.

Other tales here might be more aptly called "stories of sudden awakenings", accounts of people finally facing some harsh reality either private or communal.

The old Roman proverb, *in vino veritas*, comes to mind as you read these stories. The idea of truth being revealed via alcohol has been used by these authors in different ways. The truths revealed may be positive and helpful or negative and depressing. Sometimes they are a simple recognitions of the inevitability of our lives and the inescapable consequences of our personalities, circumstances and decisions.

The most poignant story of self-realisation, for me, is "Miners' Holiday". This story is a sort of reverse of that classic Aussie novel by Kenneth Cook, *Wake in Fright*.

In *Wake in Fright* the central character realises he is trapped in a hostile, alcoholic world of brutish, outback, macho behaviour but, in "Miners' Holiday", the narrator comes to realise that he belongs with his boozy workmates in the inland mining town he previously assumed was a temporary home. His old city and coastal haunts are now an alien environment

Gavin Casey's writing has often been compared to Lawson's. The melancholy undertones in his well-crafted and observed stories of mateship and hardship are certainly reminiscent of Lawson. I think "Miners' Holiday" represents Casey's craft at its best and I find it a very sad and chilling story.

Some of these stories of awakening are quite light-hearted accounts of group behaviour. In Jacqueline Kent's "The Final Meeting of the Book Club", alcohol helps Caroline confront a truth known to all the other characters. In "When Sexy Rex Cleared the Bar" an accepted belief is thrown into doubt, resulting in a small community's loss of faith in a quite trivial, but long-held local "fact".

Perhaps the gentlest and most human displays of understanding and enlightenment come in the two Lawson stories where the narrator, Mitchell, displays, in his rambling campfire anecdotes, a true understanding of man's relationship with "the grog" and a very human acceptance of the true nature of the Australian male.

Lawson spent thousands of words attempting to make sense of the Aussie male's faltering efforts to come to terms with women. In "The Boozers' Home", he explores the idea that alcohol can help facilitate a genuine, albeit dysfunctional, relationship.

Author and psychologist, Ronald Conway, might have had just this story in mind when he wrote, in 1976, "In Australia I have found that many men try to muffle this very real feeling of being intimidated by women ... by behaving like their wives' eldest sons. In the event of this dangerous ploy proving unendurable there is always the refuge of a regular booze-up with the boys. Suspicion of one's peers is thus temporarily dissolved in plenty of alcohol — Australia's national solvent." Now, there's an enlightening thought!

> "Drunkenness, the fruitful parent of every species of crime, is still the prevailing vice of the colony."
>
> SIR GEORGE GIPPS, 1849

# A Bush Publican's Lament
## Henry Lawson

I wish I was spifflicated before I ever seen a pub!

You see, it's this way. Suppose a cove comes along on a blazin' hot day in the drought — an' *you* ought to know how hell-hot it can be out here — an' he dumps his swag in the corner of the bar; an' he turns round an' he ses ter me, "Look here, boss, I ain't got a lonely steever on me, an' God knows when I'll git one. I've tramped ten mile this mornin', an' I'll have ter tramp another ten afore to-night. I'm expectin' ter git on shearin' with ol' Baldy Thompson at West-o'-Sunday nex' week. I got a thirst on me like a sunstruck bone, an' for God sake put up a couple o' beers for me an' my mate, an' I'll fix it up with yer when I come back after shearin'."

An' what's a feller ter do? I bin there meself, an', I put it to you! I've known what it is to have a thirst on me.

An' suppose a poor devil comes along in the jim-jams, with every inch on him jumpin' an' a look in his eyes like a man bein' murdered an' sent ter hell, an' a whine in his voice like a whipped cur, an' the snakes a-chasing of him; an' he hooks me with his finger ter the far end o' the bar, as if he was goin' ter tell me that the world was ended, an' he hangs over the bar an' chews me lug, an' tries to speak, an' breaks off inter a sort o' low shriek, like a terrified woman, an' he says, "For Mother o' Christ's sake, giv' me a drink!" An' what am I to do? I bin there meself. I knows what the horrors is. He mighter blued his cheque at the last shanty. But what am I ter do? I put it ter you. If I let him go he might hang hisself ter the nex' leanin' tree.

What's a drink? Yer might arst, I don't mind a drink or two; but when it comes to half a dozen in a day it mounts up, I can tell yer. Drinks is sixpence here, I have to pay for it, an' pay carriage on it. It's all up ter me in the end. I used sometimes ter think it was lucky I wasn't west o' the sixpenny line, where I'd lose a shillin' on every drink I give away.

An' a straight chap that knows me gets a job to take a flock o' sheep or a mob o' cattle ter the bloomin' Gulf, or South Australia, or somewheers, an' loses one of his horses goin' out ter take charge, an' borrers eight quid from me ter buy another. He'll turn up agen in a year or two an' most likely want ter make me take twenty quid for that eight, an' make everybody about the place blind drunk, but I've got ter wait, an' the wine an' sperit merchants an' the brewery won't. They know I can't do without liquor in the place.

An' lars' rain Jimmy Nowlett, the bullick driver, gets bogged over his axle trees back there on the Blacksoil Plains between two flooded billerbongs, an' prays till the country steams an' his soul's busted, an' his throat like a lime kiln. He taps a keg o' rum or beer ter keep his throat in workin' order. I don't mind that at all, but him an' his mates git floodbound for near a week, an' broach more kegs, an' go on a howlin' spree in ther mud, an' spill mor'n they swipe, an' leave a tarpaulin off a load, an' the flour gets wet, an' the sugar runs out of the bags like syrup, an', what's a feller ter do? Do yer expect me to set the law onter Jimmy? I've knowned him all my life, an' he knowed my father afore I was born. He's been on the roads this forty year till he's as thin as a rat, and as poor as a myall black; an' he's got a family ter keep back there in Bourke. No, I have ter pay for it in the end, an' it all mounts up, I can tell yer.

An' suppose some poor devil of a new chum black sheep comes along, staggerin' from one side of the track to the other, and spoutin' poetry; dyin' o' heat or fever, or heartbreak an' homesickness, or a life o' disserpation he'd led in England, an' without a sprat on him, an' no claim on the Bush; an' I ketches him in me arms as he stumbles inter the bar, an' he wants me ter hold him up while he turns English inter Greek for me. An' I put him ter bed, an' he gits worse, an' I have ter send the buggy twenty mile for a doctor — an' pay him. An' the jackaroo gits worse, an' has ter be watched an' nursed an' held down sometimes; an' he raves about his home an' mother in England, an' the blarsted university that he was eddicated at, an' a woman, an' somethin' that sounds like poetry in French; an' he upsets my missus a lot, an' makes her blubber. An' he dies, an' I have ter pay a man ter bury him (an' knock up a sort o' fence round the grave arterwards ter keep the stock out), an' send the buggy agen for a parson, an', well, what's a man ter do? I couldn't let him wander away an' die like a dog in the scrub, an' be shoved underground like a dog, too, if his body was ever found. The government might pay ter bury him, but there ain't never been a pauper funeral from my house yet, an' there won't be one if I can help it, except it be meself.

An' then there's the bother goin' through his papers to try an' find out who he was an' where his friends is. An' I have ter get the missus to write a letter to his people, an' we have ter make up lies about how he died ter make it easier for 'em. An' goin' through his letters, the missus comes across a portrait an' a locket of hair, an' letters from his mother an' sisters an' girl; an' they upset her, an' she blubbers agin, an' gits sentimental, like she useter long ago when we was first married.

There was one bit of poetry, I forgit it now, that that there jackaroo kep' sayin' over an' over agen till it buzzed in me head; an', weeks after, I'd ketch the missus metterin' it to herself in the kitchen till I thought she was goin' ratty.

An' we gets a letter from the jackaroo's friends that puts us to a lot more bother. I hate havin' anythin' to do with letters. An' someone's sure to say he was lambed down an' cleaned out an' poisoned with bad bush liquor at my place. It's almost enough ter make a man wish there *was* a recordin' angel.

An' what's the end of it? I got the blazin' bailiff in the place now! I can't shot him out because he's a decent, hard-up, poor devil from Bourke, with consumption or somethin', an' he's been talking to the missus about his missus an' kids; an' I see no chance of gittin' rid of him, unless the shearers come along with their cheques from West-o'-Sunday nex' week and act straight by me. Like as not I'll have ter roll up me swag an' take the track meself in the end. They say publicans are damned, an' I think so, too; an' I wish I'd bin operated on before ever I seen a pub.

> "I always keep a supply of stimulant handy in case I see a snake —
> which I also keep handy."
>
> W.C. FIELDS, 1930

# Snakes and Alcohol
## Kenneth Cook

"There's two things that don't mix," said Blackie slowly and pompously, "snakes and alcohol."

It would never have occurred to me to mix them but I nodded solemnly. Nod solemnly is pretty well all you can do when you're talking to a snake man because they never actually converse — they just tell you things about snakes.

Blackie was a travelling snake man. He travelled in a huge pantechnicon which had wooden covers on the sides. Whenever he found a paying audience — a school or a tourist centre — he would drop the wooden covers and reveal a glass-walled box the size of a large room. This was his snake house, inhabited by a hundred or so snakes ranging from the deadly taipans and browns to the harmless tree snakes.

Blackie was like all the snake men I've ever met, cadaverously thin, very dirty, extremely shabby and without a second name. I think he was called Blackie because of his fondness for black snakes, or perhaps because his eyes were jet black — he had the only eyes I've seen that were black. He looked as though his enormous pupils had supplanted his irises, but if you looked closely you could see the faint outline of the black pupils inside them. I tended to feel uncomfortable looking into those two round patches of black and the suffused and bloodshot eyes (all snake men have suffused and bloodshot eyes — I think it's because snakes bite them so often).

I met Blackie just north of Mackay in Queensland where we were both camping on a little known beach named Macka's Mistake; I don't know why it's named that. I was trying to finish a novel and Blackie was doing something complicated with the air conditioning of his pantechnicon, so we were thrown together for about a fortnight and became firm friends.

Blackie was so good and confident with snakes that he imbued me with much of his own attitude. I would often go into his snake house, sit on a log and talk to him while lethal reptiles regarded us torpidly within striking distance or slid gracefully and slowly away from the smell of our tobacco smoke.

Now and then a black, brown or green snake would slide softly past my foot and Blackie would say, "Just sit there and don't move. It won't bite you if you don't move." I wouldn't move and the snake wouldn't bite me. So, after a time, I became more or less relaxed with the snakes, provided Blackie was there.

Nothing would have induced me to go into the snake cage without Blackie, but I was convinced he could actually talk to the things, or at any rate communicate with them in some way which both he and they understood. It seemed to me at times fancifully possible that Blackie might have some drops of snake blood in his veins. Or perhaps the venom he had absorbed made him somehow *simpatico* with the creatures. Mind you, I did notice that the snakes had black eyes too, and that made me wonder.

There was only one other camper at Macka's beach, Alan Roberts, a fat and friendly little photographer who had set up a tent and was making a study of seabirds. He, Blackie and I would usually meet in my campervan for drinks in the evening.

Only the previous night, Blackie had been expounding to me and Alan the dangers of mixing alcohol and snakes. Of course, this took place over a bottle of whisky and I was considerably disconcerted when I called on him in the morning to find him unconscious in his own snake house, two empty whisky bottles by his side and his body festooned with deadly snakes.

The snakes were lying quite still, apparently enjoying the warmth of Blackie's motionless body. I assumed he was alive because of the snores that shook the glass windows of the snake house. But I had no idea whether he had been bitten and was in a coma, or had simply drunk himself insensible, or both.

The snakes resting on Blackie were, as far as I could make out: one taipan (absolutely deadly) two king browns (almost as deadly) a death adder (very deadly) three black snakes (deadly) and one diamond snake (harmless).

My first impulse was to run screaming for help, but there was nobody in sight, and if Blackie jerked or turned in his drunken or moribund torpor, at least seven deadly snakes would probably sink their fangs into him simultaneously. Then, no doubt, the other eighty or ninety variably venomous snakes would stop lying peacefully round the snake house and join the fray. Blackie's chances of survival would be slight.

I knew the snake house door did not lock. Normally when not in use it was covered by a wooden shutter, so I knew I could get in. But did I want to?

I didn't consider that in his present state Blackie would be able to provide his normal protection against snakes. Going in with Blackie like this would be worse than going in alone. A treacherous voice within me whispered that it would be better to run away and let Blackie wake up naturally. The snakes were used to him and he would probably instinctively act in the proper way with them.

Sadly, the treacherous voice wasn't convincing. Besides, I didn't know whether Blackie had already been bitten and needed medical help urgently.

I looked around for a weapon. Under the pantechnicon I saw a rake that Blackie used for clearing his snake house. I picked it up and cautiously and very slowly opened the door. There were several snakes between me and Blackie and I wasn't sure of their species. They all looked lethal. I poked at them gently with the rake and all of them, except one, resentfully slithered off to the other side of the snake house with no apparent intention except of going back to sleep. The one, a big king brown, raised itself on its coils and began hissing, throwing its head back to strike. I knew enough about snakes now to know that as long as I stayed the length of the snake's body away from its fangs, they couldn't reach me. Equally I knew that if I tried to pass this snake to get at Blackie, it could get to me.

I poked at it with the rake again and it struck, its fangs making a tiny ringing sound against the iron prongs. Blackie had told me that this sort of thing was bad for a snake's fangs. I didn't care. I poked at it again and it sank to the ground, wriggled over to Blackie, worked its way onto his back, then coiled again and began looking at me threateningly. It seemed much more agitated than before; no doubt its teeth hurt. The snakes already using Blackie as a mattress stirred fitfully, but didn't go anywhere.

A black snake detached itself from a group near the wall and came towards me. I banged it with the rake and it retired, probably mortally hurt. Again, I didn't care.

The king brown was hissing like a leaking steam pipe and the death adder appeared to dislike this. It made its way off, taking a path over Blackie's motionless head. There were still eight snakes on Blackie, seven of which were deadly.

I pushed tentatively at the king brown and it reared back, but didn't strike again. The movement disturbed the diamond snake and it went off to a quieter place. But that wasn't any real advantage, as it was harmless anyway.

A couple more black snakes started circling the walls and I remembered that the door behind me was open. There was a reasonable chance that within minutes the population of the snake house would be ravening around Macka's Mistake beach. I preferred they should escape rather than remain in the snake house with me, but I didn't want them waiting just outside when, if ever, I managed to drag Blackie through the door. I banged the rake on the floor in front of them. They stopped, considered this phenomenon, then retreated. I went back and pushed the door almost to.

What was Blackie's great maxim about snakes? Handle them very gently and slowly and they'll never bite you. I eyed the waving, hissing, tongue-flicking king brown on Blackie's back and decided I didn't believe this. Possibly if this king brown would just vacate Blackie's back I might be able to prod the rest away, gently and slowly.

However, the king brown showed no inclination to move and it was so angry now I felt that if Blackie so much as twitched an ear it would have him. I was sweating with terror and the rake handle was slippery in my grasp. The tension in my body was so great I knew that if I didn't solve this quickly I would collapse or run weeping from the snake house.

The devil with treating snakes slowly and gently, I thought; you can also treat them quickly and violently. I swung the rake at the weaving king brown with every intention of decapitating it if possible. It ducked. The rake missed. The snake struck. It became entangled with the prongs and I was holding the rake in the air with the king brown on the end of it. It sorted itself out quickly, coiled itself around the handle of the rake and began moving towards my hands. Convulsively I flung the rake away. It fell flat on Blackie's body, stirring the current inhabitants into a frenzy.

Fortunately, they all seemed to think they were being attacked by other snakes. They whipped up onto their coils and began threatening each other. Then, presumably trying for more advantageous positions, they all slipped off Blackie and began retreating towards the walls. Only one, the taipan, came near me.

All I could do was try the standard procedure of not moving and hope it would not notice that I was trembling uncontrollably. It went past and took up a position near the door.

Blackie was clear of snakes for the moment. He still hadn't moved. But now seemed safe to try to wake him.

"Blackie!" I screamed and prodded him with my foot. He didn't stir. "Blackie!" I screamed again and kicked him hard in the ribs. He still didn't stir.

All the snakes were awake and active now, but inclined to stay near the walls. The only immediate problem was the taipan against the almost-closed door. Obviously there was no chance of rousing Blackie, so I leaned down and grabbed him by the shoulders. He half turned and belched. The alcohol-loaded gust of breath was the only thing I have ever encountered to approach a camel's breath for sheer noxiousness. The rake was still across Blackie's back. I grabbed it with one hand and grabbed him by the collar with the other.

The collar came away in my hand. I grabbed him by his sparse hair, but there wasn't enough of it to get a good hold. I grabbed him by the back of his shirt. A great patch of it came away, revealing a bony, dirty yellow back. There was not much left to grab him by, so I took him by the hand and began hauling. Fortunately the hand held together.

Blackie was no great weight and I began inching him across the floor, brandishing the rake at the taipan guarding the door and desperately aware of the sea of serpents to my right and left and behind me.

A carpet snake, quite harmless, wriggled within a handspan of my right foot and I hit it with the rake out of sheer spite. I was close to the door, just out of range of the taipan, which showed no sign of moving. I pushed at it with the rake but it ducked disdainfully and stayed where it was, weaving slowly and keeping its evil eyes fixed, I was sure, on my bare, exposed and palpitating throat.

I was desperately tempted to throw Blackie at the taipan and probably would have done, except that it's hard to throw a man anywhere when you've only got him by the hand.

I had, of course, been bellowing my head off for help for some minutes now and it came in the form of Alan Roberts, the photographer who, seeing through the plate glass what was happening, gallantly flung open the door to come to my help.

The violently pushed door caught the taipan fair in the back of the neck and squashed it against the wall. I went through the door, hauling Blackie after me.

"What the bloody hell ...?" Alan was saying.

Blackie had somehow stuck on the steps of the snake house. The taipan apparently undamaged by the door, was very close to his exposed ankle, which it was inspecting curiously. The other snakes were mercifully milling some distance away, hissing among themselves.

"Help me get him out!" I gasped. Alan went through my routine of trying to grab Blackie by the collar, hair and back of shirt and ended up with handfuls of collar, hair and shirt before he grabbed Blackie's other hand. Together we hauled him through the door and slammed it in the face of the taipan, which seemed anxious to follow.

Blackie folded into a grubby heap on the ground and I leaned against the glass and tried to start breathing, which I had apparently stopped doing some time before.

"Has he been bitten?" said Alan.

"I don't know," I croaked. "Get an ambulance."

Alan, a competent man who was not about to ask foolish questions, turned to go. Blackie jackknifed to his feet, opened the door of the snake house and tried to go back in.

Alan and I grabbed him by the shoulders and slammed the door.

"Blackie!" shouted Alan. "What's wrong with you?"

Blackie, immobilised, stared at the closed door bemusedly.

"He's very drunk," I said. "I don't know whether he's been bitten or not." I was beginning to doubt it. I didn't think people came out of snake poison comas quite so abruptly. If he was out of a coma.

"Blackie," I said, "are you awake? Has a snake bitten you?"

Blackie focused on me and said disdainfully, "Snakes don't bite me."

"I think he's just drunk," I said quietly to Alan, and then to Blackie, "better come up to my campervan and lie down for a while, Blackie."

"Sure," said Blackie, "just lie down in here." And he turned and tried to get in with the snakes again. Alan and I grabbed him.

"Come on, Blackie, come up to the van and have a sleep."

But Blackie had looked through the plate glass and seen his beloved snakes rushing backwards and forwards or coiled and waving and hissing.

"Something's wrong with my snakes!" he roared, and began to struggle with us to get free.

"Blackie, Blackie," said Alan, "take it easy. You've had a few drinks …"

"'Course I've had a few drinks," said Blackie. "Can't a man have a few drinks?"

"Of course you can, Blackie," I said soothingly, "but you were passed out with snakes all over you. We just hauled you out."

Blackie looked at me closely. "So that's why my snakes are all upset," he said.

"That's right, Blackie."

Blackie thought about that. "Ah well," he said after a while, "I suppose you meant no harm. Don't do it again, though."

And the wretched man pulled away and tried to get in the door again. Alan and I could hold him easily, but we weren't prepared to do it indefinitely.

"Now listen, Blackie," I said firmly, "just come over to my van and have a few hours' sleep and you can come back to your snakes."

"I'm going back to my snakes now," said Blackie. "Get your hands off me."

We let him go, but Alan slipped between him and the door. Blackie considered this new problem.

"I'm going in there," he said quietly and threateningly.

"Calm down, Blackie," said Alan reasonably.

Blackie took a wild and ineffectual swipe at him. Alan and I looked at each other helplessly. I mouthed the word "Police?" behind Blackie's back and Alan nodded regretfully.

"Can you keep him out of there?" I asked.

"Yes," said Alan confidently. I thought he could, too; Blackie was far too drunk to put up much of a fight.

The trouble was I didn't know where the nearest telephone was. As far as I knew I might have to go into Mackay, eighty kilometres away.

I drove at incredible speed down to the highway and was delighted to see a police patrol car go past at the junction of the roads. I sped after it with my hand on the horn and it stopped. I leaped out of my van and ran to the police care. Two solemn Queensland policemen, both fat, red-faced, without humour, eternally middle-aged, looked at me expressionlessly.

"I wonder, would you follow me?" I said breathlessly. "I've got a friend who's very drunk and who wants to sleep with his snakes."

There was a long pause.

"What?" said the two policemen eventually, simultaneously.

"I've got a friend who's very drunk who wants to sleep with his snakes," I said again, but this time I could hear my own words.

There was another long pause.

"Could you explain a bit more, sir?" said the driver policeman. Even then I could wonder at the talent of policemen for using the word "sir" as an insult.

"Oh the hell with it, it's too difficult to explain. Just follow me, will you? It's urgent."

I thought they probably would follow me, if not necessarily for the reason I wanted them to. I was right. They did and we arrived back at Macka's Mistake to find Blackie pinned to the ground with Alan Roberts kneeling on his shoulders. The snake house was still a whirl of activity. Blackie was shouting obscenities with considerable eloquence.

I don't say the policemen put their hands on their guns, but they looked as though they might any minute.

It was all too difficult to explain, so I just gestured at the strange tableau of Blackie and Alan in front of the snake house.

"What seems to be the problem?" said one of the policemen.

Blackie stopped shouting when he saw the uniforms. Alan let him go and he stood up, stared for a moment then looked reproachfully and unbelievingly at me. "You called the cops," he accused.

"What is all this?" said the policeman.

Blackie saved the necessity for an explanation by feebly trying to punch the policeman's nose. They took him off to Mackay and charged him with being drunk and disorderly.

Alan and I waited through the day until we felt he must be reasonably sober and then went down and bailed him out.

Blackie was silent until halfway through the journey back when he suddenly and tearfully asked, "How could you do this to me?"

Alan and I explained the sequence of events to him.

"Is that true?" he said.

"Perfectly true, Blackie. We had to do it."

"I can see that. Funny, I don't remember any of it."

I tactfully made no reference to the two empty bottles of whisky.

"I'm really sorry," Blackie said. "Just goes to show, though, snakes and alcohol don't mix."

> "The governor, clergy, officers civil and military, all ranks and
> descriptions of people bartered spirits when I left the colony."
>
> CAPT. KEMP, NSW CORPS, 1815

# Court Day at Billy Billy
## Anonymous (The *Bulletin* 1896)

The court house interior was almost bare of furniture, the walls
were unlined and the weather-boards gaped here and there, so
that the grasshoppers jumped in and out at their pleasure. Their
worships (two of them) sat on a small form behind a pine table,
the prisoner hung over a deal railing about eighteen inches from
the wall, and Constable O'Toole stood near, reciting the villainies
of the accused in a thick, monotonous, unintelligible brogue.

It was a day in Gehenna: the shrill, ringing whirr of the locusts
filled the air for miles around, a bird chipped its beak sharply on
the iron roof, and a tall, attenuated goat stood in the doorway,
supinely observing the proceedings of the court, and emitting an
occasional contemptuous "bah".

But the court seemed oblivious to everything but the dreadful
heat and its own sorrows. Half of the court, open-mouthed,
followed the meanderings of a lame bullant on the table, between
intervals of sleep, and occasionally stirred the insect up with a straw
to add to the excitement. The other half, with his head thrown back
and his occiput resting on the chair rail, gazed meditatively at the
roof, daydreaming of strong drinks and occasionally relapsing into
a gurgling snore suggestive of a frog croaking in a ship's hold, and
then pulling himself together with an effort and trying to look wise.

And all the time Constable O'Toole droned along about "this
yere mahn" who had been discovered the night previous, howling

on the road "afore widdy Johnson's," with nothing on, "barrin' th' dust, yer worships, which he'd buried hisself in."

Prisoner was charged with drunkenness and disorderly conduct, and was a woebegone object, the Sahara incarnate. His tongue could be heard grating against his palate and he looked piteously thirsty. When the policeman had done, he put in a word or two in extenuation of his weakness, reminding their worships of the weather they had been having, and concluding with a touching and wholly ineffectual effort to expectorate.

The court felt itself called upon, and one half arose, and, steadying itself by leaning over the table, assumed a look of inhuman gravity, and said: "Prisoner, such conducksh wholly indefenshible — disgrash tyer manhood. Your are fined sheven daysh or twenty-four hoursh."

Then that half sat down, with the air of a man who has done his duty by his country, and the other half arose, and, after blinking for a few moments at the prisoner, with an assumption of owl-like wisdom, added: "Sheven daysh 'r twenty-foursh hoursh, *both of you!*"

"Yesh," corroborated the first half, rising again, "*both of you!*"

Then the court adjourned.

> "This is, perhaps, the golden rule, no woman should marry a teetotaller, or a man who does not smoke."
>
> ROBERT LOUIS STEVENSON, 1881

# The Boozers' Home
## Henry Lawson

"A dipsomaniac," said Mitchell, "needs sympathy and commonsense treatment.

"Now, I'm not taking the case of a workman who goes on the spree on pay night and sweats the drink out of himself at work next day, nor a slum-bred brute who guzzles for the love of it; but a man with brains, who drinks to drown his intellect or his memory. He's generally a man under it all, and a sensitive, generous, gentle man with finer feelings as often as not. The best and cleverest in the world seem to take to drink mostly. It's an awful pity. Perhaps it's because they're straight and the world's crooked and they can see things too plain. And I suppose in the Bush the loneliness and the thoughts of the girl-world they left behind help to sink 'em.

"Now a drunkard seldom reforms at home, because he's always surrounded by the signs of the ruin and misery he has brought on the home; and the sight and thought of it set him off again before he's had time to recover from the last spree. Then, again, the noblest wife in the world mostly goes the wrong way to work with a drunken husband, nearly everything she does is calculated to irritate him. If, for instance, he brings a bottle home from the pub, it shows that he wants to stay at home and not go back to the pub any more, but the first thing that the wife does is to get hold of the bottle and plant it, or smash it before his eyes, and that maddens him in the state he is in then.

"No. A dipsomaniac needs to be taken away from home for a while. I knew a man that got so bad that the way he acted at home one night frightened him, and next morning he went into an inebriate home of his own accord, to a place where his friends had been trying to get him for a year past. For the first day or two he was nearly dead with remorse and shame, mostly shame; and he didn't know what they were going to do to him next, he only wanted them to kill him quick and be done with it. He reckons he felt as bad as if he was in gaol. But there were ten other patients there, and one or two were worse than he was, and that comforted him a lot. They compared notes and sympathised and helped each other. They discovered that all their wives were noble women.

"He struck one or two surprises too — one of the patients was a doctor who'd attended him one time, and another was an old boss of his, and they got very chummy. And there was a man there who was standing for parliament — he was supposed to be having a rest down the coast ... Yes, my old mate felt very bad for the first day or two; it was all *Yes, nurse*, and *Thank you, nurse*, and *Yes, doctor,* and *No, doctor*, and *Thank you, doctor.* But, inside a week, he was calling the doctor "Ol' Pill-Box" behind his back, and making love to one of the nurses.

"But he said it was pitiful when women relatives came to visit patients the first morning. It shook the patients up a lot, but I reckon it did 'em good. There were well-bred old lady mothers in black, and hard-working, haggard wives and loving daughters, and the expressions of sympathy and faith and hope in those women's faces! My old mate said it was enough in itself to make a man swear off drink forever ... Ah, God, what a world it is!

"Reminds me how I once went with the wife of another old mate of mine to see him. He was in a lunatic asylum. It was about the worst hour I ever had in my life, and I've had some bad ones. The way she tried to coax him back to his old self. She thought she could do it when all the doctors had failed. But I'll tell you about him some other time.

"The old mate said that the principal part of the treatment was supposed to be injection of bichloride of gold or something, and it was supposed to be a secret. It might have been water and sugar for all he knew, and he thought it was. You see, when patients got better they were allowed out, two by two, on their honour, one to watch the other — and it worked. But it was necessary to have an extra hold on them; so they were told that if they were a minute late for 'treatment' or missed one injection, all the good would be undone. This was dinged into their ears all the time. Same as many things are done in the Catholic religion — to hold the people.

"My old mate said that, as far as the medical treatment was concerned, he could do all that was necessary himself. But it was the sympathy that counted, especially the sympathy between the patients themselves. They always got hold of a new patient and talked to him and cheered him up; he nearly always came in thinking he was the most miserable wretch in this world. And it comforts a man and strengthens him and makes him happier to meet another man who's worse off or sicker, or has been worse swindled than he has been. That's human nature … And a man will take draughts from a nurse and eat for her when he wouldn't do it for his own wife, not even though she had been a trained nurse herself. And if a patient took a bad turn in the night at the Boozers' Home and got up to hunt the snakes out of his room he wouldn't be sworn at, or laughed at, or held down; no, they'd help him shoo the snakes out and comfort him. My old mate said that, when he got better, one of the new patients reckoned that he licked St Patrick at managing snakes. And when he came out he didn't feel a bit ashamed of his experience.

"The institution didn't profess to cure anyone of drink, only to mend up shattered nerves and build up wrecked constitutions; give them back some willpower if they weren't too far gone. And they set my old mate on his feet all right. When he went in his life seemed lost, he had the horror of being sober, he couldn't start the day without a drink or do any business without it. He couldn't live for more than two hours without a drink, but when he came out he didn't feel as if he wanted it. He reckoned that those six weeks in the institution were the happiest he'd ever spent in his life, and he wished the time had been longer; he says he'd never met with so much sympathy and genius, and humour and human nature under one roof before. And he said it was nice and novel to be looked after and watched and physicked and bossed by a pretty nurse in uniform — but I don't suppose he told his wife that. And when he came out he never took the trouble to hide the fact that he'd been in. If any of his friends had a drunkard in the family, he'd recommend the institution and do his best to get him into it. But when he came out he firmly believed that if he took one drink he'd be a lost man. He made a mania of that.

"One curious effect was that, for some time after he left the institution, he'd sometimes feel suddenly in high spirits, with nothing to account for it — something like he used to feel when he had half a dozen whiskies in him; then suddenly he'd feel depressed and sort of hopeless, with nothing to account for that either, just as if he was suffering a recovery. But those moods never lasted long and he soon grew out of them altogether. He didn't flee temptation. He'd knock round the pubs on Saturday nights with his old mates, but never drank anything but soft stuff; he was always careful to smell his glass for fear of an accident or a trick. He drank gallons of ginger-beer, milk-and-soda and lemonade; and he got very fond of sweets, too; he'd never liked them before.

"He said he enjoyed the novelty of the whole thing and his mates amused him at first; but he found he had to leave them early in the evening, and, after a while, he dropped them altogether. They seemed such fools when they were drunk (they'd never seemed fools to him before). And, besides, as they got full, they'd get suspicious of him, and then mad at him, because he couldn't see things as they could.

"That reminds me that it nearly breaks a man's heart when his old drinking chum turns teetotaller, it's worse than if he got married or died. When two mates meet and one is drunk and the other sober, there is only one of two things for them to do if they want to hit it together, either the drunken mate must get sober or the sober mate drunk.

"And that reminds me: Take the case of two old mates who've been together all their lives, say they always had their regular sprees together and went through the same stages of drunkenness together, and suffered their recoveries and sobered up together, and each could stand about the same quantity of drink and one never got drunker than the other. Each, when he's boozing, reckons his mate the cleverest man and the hardest case in the world, second to himself.

"But one day it happens, by a most extraordinary combination of circumstances, that Bill, being sober, meets Jim very drunk, and pretty soon Bill is the most disgusted man in this world. He never would have dreamed that his old mate could make such a fool and such a public spectacle of himself. And Bill's disgust intensifies all the time he is helping Jim home, and Jim arguing with him and wanting to fight him, and slobbering over him and wanting to love him by turns, until Bill swears he'll give Jim a hammering as soon as ever he's able to stand steady on his feet."

"I suppose your old boozing mate's wife was very happy when he reformed," I said to Mitchell.

"Well, no," said Mitchell, rubbing his head rather ruefully. "I suppose it was an exceptional case. But I knew her well, and the fact is that she got more discontented and thinner, and complained and nagged him worse than she'd ever done in his drinking days. And she'd never been afraid of him. Perhaps it was this way: she loved and married a careless, good-natured, drinking scamp, and when he reformed and became a careful, hard-working man, and an honest and respected fellow-townsman, she was disappointed in him. He wasn't the man that won her heart when she was a girl. Or maybe he was only company for her when he was half drunk. Or maybe lots of things. Perhaps he'd killed the love in her before he reformed — and reformed too late. I wonder how a man feels when he finds out for the first time that his wife doesn't love him any longer? But my old mate wasn't the nature to find out that sort of thing.

"Ah, well! If a woman caused all our trouble, my God! Women have suffered for it since, and they suffer like martyrs mostly and with the patience of working bullocks. Any way it goes, if I'm the last man in the world and the last woman is the worst, and there's only room for one more in Heaven I'll step down at once and take my chance in Blazes."

> "Drink, sir, is a great provoker ..."
>
> SHAKESPEARE, 1606, *MACBETH* II:III

# When Sexy Rex Cleared the Bar
## Jim Haynes

Sexy Rex was a shearers' cook, or had been ... or said he had been.

When I knew him he spent most of his time *telling* people about being a shearer's cook — from a corner of the bar at the Tatts, or the Royal — or at odd times when his liver was having a bad day, from a table near the window in the Paragon Cafe. Maybe he'd never been a shearers' cook at all. I never met anyone who remembered him being one. There were plenty of people, however, who remembered him *telling* them about being one.

Being a shearers' cook doesn't seem much to boast about, or spend most of your time reminiscing about. Most blokes I know who had been shearers' cooks kept pretty quiet about it and found other things to talk about. They certainly found other things to boast about. Admitting to having been a shearers' cook was really an admission that, for one reason or another, you couldn't shear "at that point in time", as the politicians say (or "then" as anyone else would say).

Not being able to shear, at any time, usually cast a sort of shadow on a bloke's ability to shear at all, and most blokes who could shear at all didn't like that sort of doubt being cast over their ability. But Sexy Rex *liked* to boast about being a shearers' cook.

He was probably called "Sexy Rex" because he was the least sexy person imaginable, or simply because it was the first rhyme that sprang to mind — or perhaps a bit of both.

Anyway, Sexy Rex walked with a pronounced limp, when he walked at all. He didn't walk much, for two reasons. Firstly because of his pronounced limp and secondly because his main claim to fame, his real skill in life, was cadging lifts from one pub to the other, because he walked with a pronounced limp.

No one ever questioned that Rex's limp was a result of "the war". But the funny thing was that he never talked about "the war" or claimed to have fought in World War 11. He'd arrived in the district after the war, complete with his pronounced limp so I guess everyone just assumed that he acquired the limp in the war. He didn't wear an RSL badge and he didn't march in the Anzac Day parade because of his limp. He did do his share of "anzacing" at the pub after the march but his reminiscences, even on Anzac Day, were invariably about being a shearers' cook.

It was actually "Spanner" Toole who cleared the bar at the Royal, and that was because he was fed up with "Boof" Simpson and Billy O'Shea reminding him about the belting they'd given him the night before outside the town's other pub, the Tatts.

Now the hiding Spanner had copped the night before outside the Tatts was pretty much Spanner's fault. He could be fairly annoying when he tied one on and he had this bad habit of digging up a little "local history" and broadcasting it around the bar, airing other people's dirty laundry in public.

Let's be honest, Spanner was a nasty piece of work when he'd had a few. There weren't many drinkers at the Tatts who had any time for him when he was in that condition. On Friday night at the Tatts he was getting no encouragement from the other drinkers, but he expounded his theories none-the-less and anyone who was in the bar couldn't help but hear them. On this particular occasion his theory concerned the alleged results of an alleged relationship between his own father, now deceased, and Nola Simpson.

Nola Simpson was not deceased but very much alive and kicking. What's more she was Boof's mother and Billy's aunt. Boof and Billy were quite willing to do the kicking necessary to defend her honour, especially when the kickee was Spanner Toole.

By all accounts Nola's son and nephew had done a pretty good job of defending her honour in her absence outside the Tatts that night. There was a good case to argue that Spanner had gone way beyond the bounds of decency in his attack upon the honour of Nola Simpson. Boof's lineage had been brought into question by Spanner's verbal attack, so Boof himself had been maligned in a quite scurrilous manner. Spanner's assertion, logically considered, placed Boof in the position of being Spanner's half-brother. This in itself was reason enough to give Spanner a hiding, according to some. Nobody in their right mind wanted to be accused of being related to Spanner Toole.

But Spanner's drunken ravings, broadcast to the bar at maximum decibels, also cast doubt on Billy's origins. On top of all this, Spanner had quite openly invited both of them to "have a go". Therefore, one argument went, he not only deserved a hiding, but it served him right that it was meted out by the two blokes he had insulted, and then invited to give him a hiding.

Nola Simpson's sister, Maggie, was now Mrs Maggie O'Shea. She was also Billy's mother, indeed, the mother of one entire branch of the almost innumerable O'Shea family. This family, virtually unaided, kept the town's Catholic priest Father Connolly fully occupied with christenings, marriages, deaths and prison visits.

It was certainly not wise to cast aspersions, no matter how vague and passing, on anyone related to the O'Shea clan. It took a very brave man to suggest anything of the kind. Substitute "drunken and stupid" for "brave" and you'd be closer to the mark; much closer in Spanner's case.

The resulting fight outside the Tatts had, by all accounts, not been a pretty sight and Spanner was an even less pretty sight than usual when he arrived at the Royal for a recuperative drink the next day.

Boof and Billy were already drinking at the Royal when Spanner arrived; they had naturally been barred from the Tatts for giving Spanner a hiding.

Boof and Billy held no particular grudge against Dougie, the Tatts' publican, about being barred from the Tatts by Dougie, even though they had not started the fight. They pretty much accepted that, if you got involved in a Friday night "incident" and then gave someone a hiding outside a pub, you would be barred from that pub for a time. So Boof and Billy were drinking at "the other pub" and having a few bets with Fancy Youngman, the SP bookie, when Spanner arrived.

In charge of the bar that day was Harold Davis, known as "Happy Harold" to the desperate drinkers who frequented the Royal, because he never smiled. He lived alone in a bit of a shanty on the edge of town, in a bend of the river known to locals as Happy Valley. Happy Harold was a "Jimmy Woodser", a solitary drinker who was always sober when he was at work behind the bar at the Royal, and never sober any other time. He had a dry wit, told a good story and got drunk as soon as he finished a shift.

It wasn't Spanner Toole alone who cleared the bar at the Royal that Saturday afternoon, it was a combination of Spanner and the old side-by-side double-barrelled shotgun he got out from under the seat of his ute and carried back into the bar. He did this because he was fed up with Boof Simpson and Billy O'Shea insulting him and reminding him about the belting they had given him the night before outside the Tatt's.

"When Spanner and the shotgun entered the bar," Harold said later, "the bar cleared pretty quickly."

A lot of blokes disappeared into the toilets at the end of the bar. Gender was suddenly not an issue according to Harold, the Ladies being just as popular as the Gents at that particular moment. A lot of the bar cleared into the lounge and taproom at the further end. The bar did not, oddly enough, clear into the street, perhaps because the area in the general vicinity of that door was more or less occupied by Spanner and the shotgun.

Harold was left alone in the relative safety of the area behind the bar, with the glasses piled high along it. He had simply to duck down to remove the immediate threat of being in the firing line of Spanner and his shotgun.

Which brings us to the crux of the story really. It was at that point, as he ducked down, that Harold realised he was no longer alone behind the bar. He had been joined there by Sexy Rex.

Harold says that Sexy Rex, in spite of his limp and alleged "bad" leg must have *cleared the bar* and the glasses stacked on it to join him in relative safety behind it.

Were we to believe Happy Harold would tell lies? Or did we choose to believe that our local crippled ex-serviceman could clear a four-foot bar, stacked with glasses, in a split second with no apparent side effects?

It was a dilemma which would concern the town longer than the current crisis. Because Spanner stopped yelling abuse at the whole town in general, and Boof and Billy in particular, when the sergeant arrived a few minutes later to relieve him of the shotgun.

While Spanner climbed quietly into the paddy wagon to be taken to the lockup the sergeant did something quite uncharacteristic. He had Spanner's collar in one hand and the shotgun in the other and, knowing Spanner as well as he did, he assumed that Spanner would never actually *load* a shotgun and take it into the bar of the Royal. So he pointed the gun, which was cocked, at the outside brick wall of the pub, and pulled the trigger.

The marks of the pellets are still there in the brickwork today. They serve as a constant and historic reminder of Harold's amazing claim that Sexy Rex cleared the bar the day that Spanner Toole cleared the bar with the loaded shotgun.

But even Harold was forced to admit he didn't actually *see* Sexy Rex clear the bar. Perhaps Sexy Rex got behind the bar another way. None of us can imagine how, but we prefer to leave the episode in the unsolved file rather than believe that Sexy Rex was not the genuine article.

# The Guile of Dad McGinnis
## W.T. Goodge

When McGinnis struck the mining camp at Jamberoora Creek
His behaviour was appreciated highly;
For, although he was a quiet man, in manner mild and meek,
Not like ordinary swagmen with a monumental cheek,
He became the admiration of the camp along the creek
'Cause he showed a point to Kangaroobie Riley!

Both the pubs at Jamberoora had some grog that stood the test
(Not to speak of what was manufactured slyly!)
And the hostel of O'Gorman, which was called The Diggers' Rest,
Was, O'Gorman said, the finest house of any in the west;
But it was a burning question if it really was the best,
Or the Miners', kept by Kangaroobie Riley.

Dad McGinnis called at Riley's. Said he "felt a trifle queer",
And with something like a wan and weary smile, he
Said he "thought he'd try a whisky". Pushed it back and said, "I
    fear
I had better take a brandy." Passed that back and said: "Look
    here,
Take the brandy; after all, I think I'll have a pint of beer!"
And he drank the health of Kangaroobie Riley!

"Where's the money?" asked the publican; "you'll have to pay,
   begad!"
"Gave the brandy for the beer!" said Dad the wily,
"And I handed you the whisky when I took the brandy, lad!"
"But you paid not for the whisky!" answered Riley. "No," said
   Dad,
"And you don't expect a man to pay for what he never had!"
— 'Twas the logic flattened Kangaroobie Riley!

"See," said Kangaroobie Riley, "you have had me, that is clear!
But I never mind a joke," he added dryly.
"Just you work it on O'Gorman, and I'll shout another beer."
"I'd be happy to oblige yer," said McGinnis with a leer,
"But the fact about the matter is, O'Gorman sent me here!
So, good morning, Mr Kangaroobie Riley!"

**"One more drink and I'd have been under the host."**

Dorothy Parker, 1935

# The Final Meeting of the Book Club
## Jacqueline Kent

"Well," said Caroline briskly, "shall we choose the book for next time?" She paused, waiting for us to answer. When nobody did, she said: "What about something by — ooh — say, Virginia Woolf?"

Andree, Allison and I stared into our wine glasses. Jo, who was less polite, groaned.

"Not a good idea?" Caroline opened the third bottle, the verdelho Andree had brought, and carefully topped everybody up. "And why not? Allison?"

Put on the spot Allison, who liked to keep the peace whenever possible, shrivelled. "I'm not crazy about Virginia Woolf," she confessed almost in a whisper. "I know lots of people think she's wonderful, but … whenever I read anything she wrote, I always feel as if someone's going to make me write an essay."

"Nonsense!" Caroline sipped her wine. "Virginia Woolf is a classic writer. She speaks to the female condition …"

"Oh, for heaven's sake," interrupted Jo. "Virginia Woolf only *speaks to the female condition* if you happen to be an overprivileged, neurotic woman who lived in England during the 1930s and spent time with a bunch of other literary neurotics." She'd said similar things to me before, though perhaps a little more gently.

"I won't argue with you," said Caroline in a voice of steely graciousness. "I'll only tell you that you're wrong."

"Yeah?"

"This is a really nice verdelho, Andree," said Allison quickly.

"Just tell me why I'm wrong!" Jo glared at Caroline, gulped her wine and refilled. Pointedly moving the bottle out of her reach, Caroline said: "Let's not get too upset, shall we?"

"She was a bit neurotic, Virginia, I suppose," said Andree. "But a wonderful writer."

"Absolutely." Caroline added thoughtfully, "And such a lucky woman, too. She had a really, really supportive husband."

"Here we go," said Jo to me, under her breath.

"Yep," said Caroline. "He really helped her. So she could do her work, write those brilliant books. He kept the house running."

"I see," said Jo. "So you reckon that, while old Virginia was working upstairs on her fabulous prose, Leonard was putting out the garbage without being told? Yep, makes sense. And I bet he knew his way round a chop at a barbecue, too."

"Ha ha." Caroline took an angry gulp of wine. "All I'm saying is, not all of us are lucky in that respect."

The rest of us tensed, avoiding looking at each other. We knew what was coming.

"It's not as if I ask Hugh to do much," said Caroline in what she clearly thought was a reasonable tone. "I know he works hard too. It's just ... I wish he'd help me round the house. Just a bit more."

"But don't you think most men are like that?" asked Andree. "Or most men over thirty, anyway? I mean, Bob for instance ..."

"Bob is a *saint* compared with Hugh," declared Caroline. "Anybody is. Even David."

"Thanks," said Jo.

"Hugh will never do anything off his own bat," said Caroline. "And he has to make a point about everything I ask him. He can't just mow the lawn, paying attention to the borders, like normal people. Oh no, he has to get my nail scissors and a ruler and make sure I see him measuring every blade of grass ..."

She finished her wine and poured another glass. "I think it's true. Men are from Mars. God knows I've learned to live with most of the weird things Hugh does, even the way he eats tomatoes, but ..."

"Speaking of weird," said Andree quickly, "have you ever noticed how men always know the latest sports results, even though you know they haven't read the paper or watched TV or turned the radio on? They just *know*."

"Messages through the ether from Planet Sport," suggested Jo. We laughed, except Caroline.

"Don't talk to me about sport!" she cried. "I just want Hugh to spend more time around the house. Is that too much to ask?"

"You're not serious," said Jo. "You really want him to stop earning squillions putting up office buildings and spend more time at home? You're always telling us how much you like having your own space when you need it."

"Thass true," admitted Caroline. "But I'd just like him to take more of an interest in what I do, 'stead of going on about his boring sport, sport, sport all the time. He could be more innerested in this book group, 'frinstance. I tried to tell him about the last book we did, by that French writer. Col ... Col ..."

"Colette," said Allison.

"Yup." Caroline waved her arm, narrowly missing Andree's full glass. "How come French people only have one name? Mmm? Anyway, I liked that book. It's sooooo romantic. And I told Hugh that she's a writer who really knows the *heart* of a woman. The *heart* of a woman," she repeated, and her eyes went all misty. "And you know what he said?" Pause for effect. "He said he thought Colette was an Argentinian soccer player."

"That really surprises me." Allison was beginning to have a little trouble with consonants. "Hugh's an intelligent man."

"Ha!" Caroline pulled the cork out of the fifth bottle with a vicious *plok*.

"Well, he is," said Andree. "I mean, he reads, goes to movies ..."

"I'm sure he's a romantic in his own way," added Allison.

"Pig's arse," said Caroline surprisingly. "Lemme tell you what he did the other night. We got out *Casablanca* on DVD, it's my absolutely favourite movie in the whooooole world, it's soooo romantic. And we got to the ending, and it's the very best bit, and I always cry …" Her voice wobbled. "And Hugh said, he actually said, he wished Ingrid Bergman'd get out of the way, so he could get a better look at the Lockheed Electra behind her."

Jo and I burst out laughing, and kept laughing for a long time.

"S'not funny!"

"Yes it is," said Jo. "Come on, Caroline. Lighten up!"

But there was no stopping Caroline. Without taking breath, she launched into a long, passionate description of her husband as one of the ten worst people in human history, who hated Sunday night costume dramas on ABC television, always went to the bathroom just after she'd announced dinner was on the table and was capable of sleeping in the same bedsheets for a year if she let him.

From time to time, one or other of us tried to deflect her. We might as well not have bothered. Hugh, she said bitterly, screamed with laughter over fart jokes, sang "Achy breaky heart" in the shower without being able to remember past the first two lines. And when first introduced to Caroline's parents, he had picked up two prawns from a platter, slid them under his top lip and pretended to be Dracula …

On and on she went, the level in the bottle dropping steadily as she spoke. Allison was slumped in her chair, her head in her hands, stirring only long enough to open the next bottle and fill all our glasses. I found the wood grain of the table to be so beautiful I almost burst into tears. Next to me, Andree was in tears because she had decided she was turning into her mother. Jo, her cheek resting on her arm, was drawing little patterns on the table with a wine-dipped finger. After twenty minutes, the only person sitting straight in her chair was Caroline.

"And ... not ... only ... that." Caroline suddenly spoke very slowly, with enormous emphasis. "I haven't even got to what he's like ... in ... bed."

"Oh, for God's sake!" I said.

"No!" Caroline held up a regal hand. "You are my oldest friends. You Have A Right To Know!"

"Please, Caroline," said Allison.

"I bet you think he's a sex machine. He thinks he's a sex machine. Well ha. And ha again." She glared at all of us in turn. "Ha!"

"We don't really want to hear this," pleaded Allison.

"Yes, you do," said Caroline. "I wanna tell you ..."

Jo suddenly sat up straight. She looked as bleary as the rest of us, but as she took a deep breath, I felt a sense of misgiving.

"Look," said Jo, "if you're gonna tell us what sex with Hugh is like, you might as well not bother. We know."

"Whaddya mean, you know?"

Jo sighed. "We've all been there, Caroline."

Andree and Allison both started to giggle.

"Whaddya mean, you've all been there?" Caroline suddenly sounded quite sober.

"Do I have to spell it out?" said Jo. "We all know, from personal experience, that Hugh is a dud in bed. Now, can we change the subject, please?"

In the terrible silence that followed, Allison poured Caroline another glass of wine.

> "Never have I seen so much enthusiasm for water — and so little of it drunk."
>
> SIR GEORGE REID, OPENING THE KALGOORLIE PIPELINE, 1903

# Miners' Holiday
## Gavin Casey

They poured Tom and me on to the Sunday train just as it started to move, and we collected our bottles and found our compartment. There were four other chaps in it, one we knew and three we didn't know. One of the strangers didn't seem to like us much, but the rest brightened up when they saw how many bottles we had. We settled down and loosened our ties and collar studs, and Tom took his shoes off and kicked them under the seat. We arranged the luggage so it wasn't in the way, and smoked and watched the dumps and smokestacks disappearing over the horizon.

"Good-bye and good riddance!" said Tom. "All you chaps goin' right to the coast?"

They said they were, and we began to talk about the city and the fields and the great times we were going to have for the next couple of weeks. It was a hot summer, and there was nothing to look at through the windows except mangy inland bush. I thought about the long rows of foamy breakers at North Beach, and we drank a couple of bottles. It was already smoky and stuffy in the carriage, and I liked the beer, but I was looking forward to the coast and thinking of yachting on the river and among the islands a few miles out.

"We'll have to look after the bottles," said Tom. "She gets a bit dry down the line in the middle of the night."

"There's a pub next stop," said one of the chaps. "If we make it quick we can nick across and get a few more there."

We got some more beer and started knocking them over quicker. A bottle with plenty of head on it sprayed over the stranger who wasn't drinking, and we thought that was the best joke ever. A bloke from the next compartment came and stood in the doorway and glared at us as if he'd like to say something. We laughed and offered him some beer, and he glared harder than ever and went away. Somebody found a pack of cards, and they started on poker, but I didn't play. I was full of beer and excitement and didn't feel like cards.

I sat there in the smoky carriage drinking more beer and listening to the wheels bump over the rail joints. I wondered how long each section of rail was and how much closer to the coast each *clankety-clank* took us. It would be great down there in the green, rainwashed country between the rolling coastal ranges and the sea. It would be good to see the rows of streets in which every house had lawns and flowers and the trees were different shapes and colours. Not like the fields, where the broad red roads are flanked by everlasting pepper-trees and picket fences.

Then they put up the sleepers, and, though the mob kept playing cards and making a row, I dozed. The rumble of the train became the roar of surf, and I was back at North Beach, riding the breakers like I used to six years ago, before we went to the fields.

When the train pulled in next morning we were all dry and a bit sick. Our holiday suits were crumpled and ugly and the luggage was heavy and covered with corners. The buildings weren't as big and fine-looking as I had remembered them, and they were a dirty smoke colour. It was as hot as hell, hotter than it had been on the fields. We walked out of the station and across the road and had a long, cool pot at the nearest pub. It was what we needed, and we had a couple more.

"Where're you blokes going to stay?" asked one of our new cobbers.

"We want to find a place at one of the beaches," I said.

"Aw, right in town's the place to stop," said someone. "Y' can always go out to the beaches, but if you live there you might as well die after dark."

"We want a spell," I said. "We won't care if it's quiet."

"Funny idea of a spell," said someone. "Wantin' to lug all his baggage another twenty miles as soon as he gets here."

"I'm stoppin' right where I am," said another chap. "I'm goin' to book a room. This pub looks good to me."

"Why don't we book in, too, Bill?" said Tom. "We can shift to the beach in a couple of days. We can have a spell here first."

"We can stick together an' have a bit of fun for a start," said someone.

It was sensible, I thought. I was tired, and I wanted a bath. There was a whole fortnight ahead. We'd collected a good bunch on the way down, and though it was hot in the streets it was cool in the pub. The beer was good, and I was hungry too. The chaps were all laughing and arguing about it, but I was too tired to argue. I just agreed. We had a couple of rounds to celebrate the fact that we were going to stay together for a while.

That pub was hard to leave. The concrete pavements get your feet when you're not used to them, and the pub was always cool. Every evening I'd think about getting out to the beach next day, but something would always interfere. On the Tuesday Pat Stanford and Johnny Josephs turned up from the fields, and the mob of us made a day of it. On the Wednesday there were thunderstorms. We trotted around the shops and we bought some stuff, but we always finished up in a pub. Tom was enjoying himself, but I got restless.

"Look here," I'd say when we got up in the mornings, "we came down here for a change, an' what are we doing? Roaming from pub to pub just like we would on the fields! We're shifting today, Tom. We'll get our things out after breakfast."

Tom would grumble a bit, but he'd agree. Then one of the other chaps would roam in, fuzzy-headed and yellow-looking.

"What a night!" he'd say. "Hell! There's so much fur on me tongue I think I must have a cat in me mouth."

"We're skipping after breakfast," I'd say. "We're off out to the beach, where they don't have any cats."

The chaps were laughing at me, I knew. Always one of them would dig out the rest and they'd decide that we had to have a drink before Tom and I left. An hour would pass in the bar, where it was quiet and cool, and then there'd be no bus for half an hour and we'd have a few somewhere else to pass the time. Someone from the fields would show up, or some bloke one of us knew at the coast. I'd check the clock and worry while they all talked and drank and made a row, but after a while I'd forget about it. We'd eat wherever we happened to be, and the money would flow out of our pockets fast and easy. And Tom and I would always land back at the pub with the mob about midnight. We made a lot of noise, but nobody minded because we spent plenty.

Then the weekend came and half our holiday was gone, and I stuck out for going to the beach.

"Christ! Why bust the party up?" said someone. "We're gettin' on all right an' havin' a good time, aren't we?"

"This's the best place in the city on Sunday," said another of them. "We're boarders, an' it's no trouble to get served."

"Why don't you all come out?" asked Tom. "Come out for the day, anyway. It'll do you good."

I didn't want them all at the beach. I only wanted Tom and me there. But they liked Tom's suggestion.

"Cripes, yes!" said someone. "We got t' see the water before we go home. Why not now?"

We got a taxi and a lot of bottles and we all piled in and went zooming off to the beach. We went through the suburbs, and I got a good look at the gardens for the first time since we'd arrived. When we were a mile from the coast I smelled the sea. Then we dropped over the last sandhills with the sound of the breakers booming away in our ears, and the car pulled up where we could see the whole beach, speckled with people and bright in the sunshine. The sand glared and hurt our eyes, but it did me good to see the beach with brown bodies all over it. There were a lot of improvements, flash pavilions and lookout towers and so on, but it was the same old beach. I remembered the first day I'd spent trying to ride a surfboard, and a lot of other occasions.

None of the chaps except Tom and I wanted to go in, but they felt they had to, and they pulled each other's legs about it until we were all in the dressing rooms. We peeled off our clothes, and I wished I'd bought a new swimming suit. Not that I'm fussy about how I look, but most of them were wearing trunks, and my old bathers were baggy as well as out-of-date. The men in the rooms were as brown as I used to be, and our mob seemed white, even their forearms and faces. You don't get sunburnt underground, or in pubs either.

When we went out the glare on the sand seemed worse, and we felt funny with our long white arms and legs and old-fashioned bathers. The sand felt funny between our naked toes, and we thought that everyone was looking at us. We hid ourselves in the water, and the water was good. Most of our mob didn't know what to do when they got in front of a "dumper", but I could still manage them, though it made me breathless. I played about for a while and then I went out past the breakers for a swim.

There was a kid with a flash stroke just ahead setting out for a buoy too. I felt good, and decided I'd see how I went against him. I put my head down and started the crawl that used to win races for me. When I looked up he was still ahead. He was looking over his shoulder, laughing. I sucked some air with a bit of unexpected wave mixed up in it, and did everything I could, until my lungs were bursting. I got another glance, and he was further ahead. The buoy was still a long way off, and my heart was hammering. My head was spinning, and I could taste sickness and beer not far from my mouth. I gave up in disgust and paddled back to the shore, where the rest of the bunch were already out and stretched on the sand.

"What a hell of a place to want to *live!*" said someone as I flopped down in the middle of them. "Golly, I'm thirsty!"

The glare from the sand was horrible, and I could feel now that there was water in my ears. We all had salt in our mouths. We all felt thirsty. The heels of kids sprinting about the beach spurned sand into our faces. When anyone looked at us we felt silly because we were too white. The water had made us tired and thirsty. We went up and dressed, and after we'd had a drink at the car we went back to town.

I felt angry with myself and disappointed. The chaps poked mullock at me, but it wasn't that that hurt. I didn't want to go near the beach again. I was quite content to be heading for the pub.

We stayed at the pub near the station with the rest for our remaining week. We saw a couple of picture shows, and every day we tramped about, bowling into a bar whenever the pavements tired our feet. We spent a lot of money, and we all used to get back to our rooms late and make a good deal of noise. It was surprising the number of other fellows from the fields we met, and we had a good time. But I wasn't sorry when the time arrived for us to get on the train again.

We took plenty of bottles, and after we'd drunk some and piled into the sleepers I lay wondering again about the length of each section of rail. Every *clankety-clank*, I thought, was carrying me a little closer to a place where I was some good, a place where there was work to be done, where I could hold my own with other men and where I didn't look funny and old-fashioned or a colour different from that of my neighbours.

> "The great advantage of a hotel is that it's a refuge from home life."
>
> GEORGE BERNARD SHAW, 1898

# The Lost Souls' Hotel
## Henry Lawson

Hungerford Road, February. One hundred and thirty miles of heavy reddish sand, bordered by dry, hot scrubs. Dense cloud of hot dust. Four wool-teams passing through a gate in a "rabbit-proof" fence which crosses the road. *Clock, clock, clock* of wheels and rattle and clink of chains, etc., crack of whips and explosions of Australian language. Bales and everything else coated with dust. Stink of old axle grease and tarpaulins. Tyres hot enough to fry chops on; bows and chains so hot that it's a wonder they do not burn through the bullocks' hide. Water lukewarm in blistered kegs slung behind the waggons. Bullocks dragging along as only bullocks do. Wheels ploughing through the deep sand, and the load lurching from side to side. Halfway on a dry stretch of seventeen miles. Big "tank" full of good water through the scrub to the right, but it is a private tank and a boundary rider is shepherding it. Mulga scrub and sparse, spiky undergrowth.

The carriers camp for dinner and boil their billies while the bullocks droop under their yokes in the blazing heat; one or two lie down and the leaders drag and twist themselves round under a dead tree, under the impression that there is shade there. The carriers look like Red Indians, with the masks of red dust "bound" with sweat on their faces, but there is an unhealthy-looking, whitish space round their eyes, caused by wiping away the blinding dust, sweat and flies. The dry sticks burn with a pale flame and an almost invisible thin pale blue smoke. The sun's heat dancing and dazzling across every white fence-post, sand-hill, or light-coloured object in the distance.

One man takes off his boot and sock, empties half a pint of sand out of them, and pulls up his trouser leg. His leg is sheathed to the knee in dust and sweat; he absently scrapes it with his knife, and presently he amuses himself by moistening a strip with his forefinger and shaving it, as if he were vaguely curious to see if he is still a white man.

The Hungerford coach ploughs past in a dense cloud of dust.

The teams drag on again like a "wounded snake that dies at sundown", if a wounded snake that dies at sundown could revive sufficiently next morning to drag on again until another sun goes down.

Hopeless-looking swagmen are met with during the afternoon, and one carrier, he of the sanded leg, lends them tobacco; his mates contribute bits o' tea, flour, and sugar.

Sundown and the bullocks done up. The teamsters unyoke them and drive them on to the next water, five miles, having previously sent a mate to reconnoitre and see that the boundary rider is not round, otherwise, to make terms with him, for it is a squatter's bore. They hurry the bullocks down to the water and back in the twilight and then, under cover of darkness, turn them into a clearing in the scrub off the road, where a sign of grass might be seen, if you look close. But the bullockies are better off than the horse teamsters, for bad chaff is sold by the pound and corn is worth its weight in gold.

Mitchell and I turned off the track at the rabbit-proof fence and made for the tank in the mulga. We boiled the billy and had some salt mutton and damper. We were making back for Bourke, having failed to get a cut in any of the sheds on the Hungerford track. We sat under a clump of mulga saplings, with our backs to the trunks, and got out our pipes. Usually, when the flies were very bad on the track, we had to keep twigs or wild turkey tail feathers going in front of our faces the whole time to keep the mad flies out of our eyes; and, when we camped, one would keep the feather going while the other lit his pipe, then the smoke would keep them away. But the flies weren't so bad in a good shade or in the darkened hut. Mitchell's pipe would have smoked out Old Nick; it was an ancient string-bound meerschaum, and strong enough to kill a blackfellow. I had one smoke out of it once when I felt bad in my inside and wanted to be sick, and the result was very satisfactory.

Mitchell looked through his old pocket-book, more by force of habit than anything else, and turned up a circular from Tattersall's. And that reminded him.

"Do you know what I'd do, Harry," he said, "if I won Tattersall's big sweep, or was to come into fifty or a hundred thousand pounds, or, better still, a million?"

"Nothing, I suppose," I said, "except to get away to Sydney or some cooler place than this."

"I'll tell you what I'd do," said Mitchell, talking round his pipe. "I'd build a Swagman's Rest right here."

"A Swagman's Rest?"

"Yes. Right here on this very God-forsaken spot. I'd build a Swagman's Rest and call it the Lost Souls' Hotel, or the Sundowners' Arms, or the Halfway House to somewhere, or some such name that would take the bushmen's fancy. I'd have it built on the best plans for coolness in a hot country; bricks, and plenty of wide verandahs with brick floors, and balconies, and shingles, in the old Australian style. I wouldn't have a sheet of corrugated iron about the place. And I'd have old-fashioned hinged sashes with small panes and vines round 'em; they look cooler and more homely and romantic than the glaring sort that shove up.

"And I'd dig a tank or reservoir for surface water as big as a lake, and bore for artesian water — and get it, too, if I had to bore right through to England; and I'd irrigate the ground and make it grow horse-feed and fruit, and vegetables too, if I had to cart manure from Bourke. And every teamster's bullock or horse, and every shearer's hack, could burst itself free, but I'd make travelling stock pay, for it belongs to the squatters and capitalists. All carriers could camp for one night only. And I'd … no, I wouldn't have any flowers; they might remind some heartbroken, new chum black sheep of the house where he was born, and the mother whose heart he broke, and the father whose grey hairs he brought down in sorrow to the grave, and break him up altogether."

"But what about the old-fashioned windows and vines?" I asked.

"Oh!" said Mitchell, "I forgot them. On second thought, I think I would have some flowers; and maybe a bit of ivy green. The new chum might be trying to work out his own salvation, and the sight of the roses and ivy would show him that he hadn't struck such a God-forgotten country after all, and help strengthen the hope for something better that's in the heart of every vagabond till he dies."

Puff, puff, puff, slowly and reflectively.

"Until he dies," repeated Mitchell. "And, maybe," he said, rousing himself, "I'd have a little room fixed up like a corner of a swell restaurant with silver and napkins on the table, and I'd fix up a waiter, so that when a broken-down university wreck came along he might feel, for a hour or so, something like the man he used to be.

"All teamsters and travellers could camp there for one night only. I'd have shower baths; but I wouldn't force any man to have a bath against his will. They could sit down to a table and have a feed off a tablecloth, and sleep in sheets, and feel like they did before their old mothers died, or before they ran away from home."

"Who? The mothers?" I asked.

"Yes, in some cases," said Mitchell. "And I'd have a nice, cool little summer house down near the artificial lake, out of earshot of the house, where the bullock drivers could sit with their pipes after tea, and tell yarns, and talk in their own language. And I'd have boats on the lake, too, in case an old Oxford or Cambridge man, or an old sailor came along, it might put years on to his life to have a pull at the oars. You remember that old sailor we saw in charge of the engine back there at the Government tank? You saw how he had the engine? Clean and bright as a new pin, everything spick and span and ship-shape, and his hut fixed up like a ship's cabin. I believe he thinks he's at sea half his time, and shoving her through it, instead of pumping muddy water out of a hole in the baking scrubs for starving stock. Or maybe he reckons he's keeping her afloat."

"And would you have fish in this lake of yours?" I asked.

"Oh, yes," said Mitchell, "and any ratty old shepherd or sundowner, that's gone mad of heat and loneliness, like the old codger we met back yonder, he could sit by the lagoon in the cool of the evening and fish to his heart's content with a string and a bent pin, and dream he's playing truant from school and fishing in the brook near his native village in England about fifty years ago. It would seem more real than fishing in the dust, as some mad old bushmen do."

"But you'd draw the line somewhere?" I asked.

"No," said Mitchell, "not even at poets. I'd try to cure them, too, with good wholesome food and plenty of physical exercise. The Lost Souls' Hotel would be a refuge for men who'd been gaolbirds once, as well as men who were gentlemen once, and for physical wrecks and ruined drunkards as well as healthy honest shearers. I'd sit down and talk to the boozer or felon just as if I thought he was as good a man as me, and he might be for that matter, God knows.

"The sick man would be kept till he recovered or died and the boozer, suffering from a recovery, I'd keep him till he was on his legs again."

"Then you'd have to have a doctor," I said.

"Yes," said Mitchell, "I'd fix all that up all right. I wouldn't bother much about a respectable medical practitioner from the city. I'd get a medical wreck who had a brilliant career before him once in England and got into disgrace, and cleared out to the colonies, a man who knows what the DTs is, a man who's been through it all and knows it all."

"Then you'd want a manager, or a clerk or secretary," I suggested.

"I suppose I would," said Mitchell. "I've got no head for figures. I suppose I'd have to advertise for him. If an applicant came with the highest testimonials of character, and especially if one was signed by a parson, I'd tell him to call again next week; and if a young man could prove that he came of a good Christian family, and went to church regularly, and sang in the choir, and taught Sunday school, I'd tell him that he needn't come again, that the vacancy was filled, for I couldn't trust him. The man who's been extra religious and honest and hardworking in his young days is most likely to go wrong afterwards. I'd sooner trust some poor old devil of a clerk who'd got into the hands of a woman or racing men when he was young, and went wrong, and served his time for embezzlement; anyway, I'd take him out and give him another chance."

"And what about woman's influence?" I asked.

"Oh, I suppose there'd have to be a woman, if only to keep the doctor on the line. I'd get a woman with a past, one that hadn't been any better than she should have been, they're generally the most kind-hearted in the end. Say an actress who'd come down in the world, or an old opera singer who'd lost her voice but could still sing a little. A woman who knows what trouble is. And I'd get a girl to keep her company, a sort of housemaid. I'd get hold of some poor girl who'd been deceived and deserted: and a baby or two wouldn't be an objection, the kids would amuse the chaps and help humanise the place."

"And what if the manageress fell in love with the doctor?" I asked.

"Well, I couldn't provide against love," said Mitchell. "I fell in love myself more than once, and I don't suppose I'd have been any worse off if I'd have stayed in love. Ah, well! But suppose she did fall in love with the doctor and marry him, or suppose the girl fell in love with the secretary? There wouldn't be any harm done; it would only make them more contented with the home and bind them to it. They'd be a happy family, and the Lost Souls' Hotel would be more cheerful and homelike that ever."

"But supposing they all fell in love with each other and cleared out," I said.

"I don't see what they'd have to clear out for," said Mitchell. "But suppose they did. There's more than one medical wreck in Australia, and more than one woman with a past, and more than one broken old clerk who went wrong and was found out, and who steadied down in gaol, and there's more than one poor girl that's been deceived. I could easily replace 'em. And the Lost Souls' Hotel might be the means of patching up many wrecked lives in that way — giving people with pasts the chance of another future, so to speak."

"I suppose you'd have music and books and pictures?" I said.

"Oh, yes," said Mitchell. "But I wouldn't have any bitter or sex problem books. They do no good. Problems have been the curse of the world ever since it started. I think one noble, kindly, cheerful character in a book does more good than all the clever villains or romantic adventurers ever invented. And I think a man ought to get rid of his maudlin sentiment in private, or when he's drunk. It's a pity that every writer couldn't put all his bitterness into one book and then burn it.

"No! I'd have good cheerful books of the best and brightest sides of human nature — Charles Dickens, and Mark Twain, and Bret Harte, and those men. And I'd have all Australian pictures — showing the brightest and best side of Australian life. And I'd have all Australian songs. I wouldn't have 'Swannie Ribber', or 'Home, Sweet Home', or 'Annie Laurie', or any of those old songs sung at the Lost Souls' Hotel — they're the cause of more heartbreaks and drink and suicide in the Bush than anything else. And if a jackeroo got up to sing 'Just before the battle, mother', or 'Mother bit me in me sleep', he'd find it was just before the battle all right. He'd have to go out and sleep in the scrub, where the mosquitoes and bulldog ants would bite him out of his sleep. I hate the man who's always whining about his mother through his nose, because, as a rule, he never cared a rap for his old mother, nor for anyone else, except his own paltry, selfish little self.

"I'd have intellectual and elevating conversation for those that …"

"Who'd take charge of that department?" I inquired hurriedly.

"Well," reflected Mitchell, "I did have an idea of taking it on myself for a while anyway; but, come to think of it, the doctor or the woman with the past would have more experience, and I could look after that part of the business at a pinch. Of course you're not in a position to judge as to my ability in the intellectual line; you see, I've had no one to practise on since I've been with you. But no matter, there'd be intellectual conversation for the benefit of black-sheep new-chums. And any broken-down actors that came alone could get up a play if they liked, it would brighten up things and help elevate the bullock drivers and sundowners. I'd have a stage fixed up and a bit of scenery. I'd do all I could to attract shearers to the place after shearing, and keep them from rushing to the next shanty with their cheques, or down to Sydney, to be cleaned out by barmaids.

"And I'd have the hero squashed in the last act for a selfish sneak, and marry the girl to the villain. He'd be more likely to make her happy in the end."

"And what about the farm?" I asked. "I suppose you'd get some expert from the agricultural college to manage that?"

"No," said Mitchell. "I'd get some poor drought-ruined selector and put him in charge of the vegetation. Only, the worst of it is," he reflected, "if you take a selector who has bullocked all his life to raise crops on dusty, stony patches in the scrubs, and put him on land where there's plenty of water and manure, and where he's only got to throw the seed on the ground and then light his pipe and watch it grow, he's apt to get disheartened. But that's human nature.

"And, of course, I'd have to have a 'character' about the place, a sort of identity and joker to brighten up things. I wouldn't get a man who'd been happy and comfortable all his life; I'd get hold of some old codger whose wife had nagged him till she died, and who'd been sold off many times, and run in for drowning his sorrows, and who started as an undertaker and failed at that, and finally got a job pottering round, gardener, or gatekeeper, or something — in a lunatic asylum. I'd get him. He'd most likely be a humorist and a philosopher, and he'd help cheer up the Lost Souls' Hotel. I reckon the lost souls would get very fond of him."

"And would you have drink at Lost Souls?" I asked.

"Yes," said Mitchell. "I'd have the best beer and spirits and wine to be had. After tea I'd let every man have just enough to make him feel comfortable and happy, and as good and clever, and innocent and honest as any other man, but no more. But if a poor devil came along in the horrors, with every inch of him jumping, and snakes, and green-eyed yahoos, and flaming-nosed bunyips chasing him, we'd take him in and give him soothing draughts, and nurse him, and watch him, and clear him out with purgatives, and keep giving him nips of good whisky, and, above all, we'd sympathise with him, and tell him that we were worse than he was many a time. We wouldn't tell him what a weak, selfish man he really was. It's remorse that hurries most men to hell, especially in the Bush. When a man firmly believes he is a hopeless case, then there's no hope for him: but let him have doubts and there's a chance. Make him believe that there are far worse cases than his. We wouldn't preach the sin of dissipation to him, no, but we'd try to show him the *folly* of a wasted life. I ought to be able to preach that, God knows.

"And, above all, we'd try to drive out of his head the cursed old popular idea that it's hard to reform — that a man's got to fight a hard battle with himself to get away from drink, pity drunkards can't believe how easy it is. And we'd put it to him straight whether his few hours' enjoyment were worth the days he had to suffer hell for it."

"And, likely as not," I said, "when you'd put him on his feet he'd take the nearest track to the next shanty, and go on a howling spree, and come back to Lost Souls' in a week, raving and worse than ever. What would you do then?"

"We'd take him in again, and build him up some more; and a third or fourth time if necessary. I believe in going right on with a thing once I take it in hand. And if he didn't turn up after the last spree we'd look for him up the scrub and bring him in and let him die on a bed, and make his death as comfortable as possible. I've seen one man die on the ground, and found one dead in the Bush. We'd bury him under a gum and put 'Sacred to the Memory of a Man who Died. Let Him R.I.P.' over him. I'd have a nice little graveyard with gums for tombstones, and I'd have some original epitaphs, I promise you."

"And how much gratitude would you expect to get out of the Lost Souls' Hotel?" I asked.

"None," said Mitchell, promptly. "It wouldn't be a Gratitude Discovery Syndicate. People might say that the Lost Souls' Hotel was a den for kidnapping women and girls to be used as decoys for the purpose of hocussing and robbing bushmen, and the law and retribution might come after me — but I'd fight the thing out. Or they might want to make a KCMG or a god of me, and worship me before they hanged me. I reckon a philanthropist or reformer is lucky if he escapes with a whole skin in the end, let alone his character. But there! Talking of gratitude: it's the fear of ingratitude that keeps thousands from doing good. It's just as paltry and selfish and cowardly as any other fear that curses the world, it's rather more selfish than most fears, in fact, take the fear of being thought a coward, or being considered eccentric, or conceited, or affected, or too good, or too bad, for instance. The man that's always canting about the world's ingratitude has no gratitude owing to him as a rule. Generally the reverse, he ought to be grateful to the world for being let live. He broods over the world's ingratitude until he gets to be a cynic. He sees moonlight shining on it and he passes on with a sour face, whereas, if he took the trouble to step inside he'd most likely find a room full of ruddy firelight, and sympathy and cheerfulness, and kindness, and love, and gratitude. Sometimes, when he's right down on his uppers, and forced to go amongst people and hustle for bread, he gets a lot of surprises at the amount of kindness he keeps running against in the world, and in places where he'd never have expected to find it. But, ah, well! I'm getting maudlin."

"And you've forgot all about the Lost Souls' Hotel," I said.

"No, I haven't," said Mitchell; "I'd fix that up all right. As soon as I'd got things going smoothly under a man I could trust, I'd tie up every penny I had for the benefit of the concern; get some 'white men' for trustees, and take the track again. I'm getting too old to stay long in one place — I'm a lost soul that always got along better in another place. I'm so used to the track that if I was shut up in a house I'd get walking up and down in my room of nights and disturb the folk; and, besides, I'd feel lost and light-shouldered without the swag."

"So you'd put all your money in the concern?"

"Yes, except a pound or two to go on the track with, for, who knows, I might come along there, dusty and tired, and ragged and hard up and old, some day, and be very glad of a night's rest at the Lost Souls' Hotel. But I wouldn't let on that I was old Mitchell, the millionaire who founded Lost Souls. They might be too officious, and I hate fuss … But it's time to take the track, Harry."

There came a cool breeze with sunset; we stood up stiffly, shouldered our swags and tucker-bags, and pushed on, for we had to make the next water before we camped. We were out of tobacco, so we borrowed some from one of the bullock drivers.

"And Noah he often said to his wife when he sat down to dine,
'I don't care where the water goes if it doesn't get into the wine.'"

G.K. CHESTERTON, 1914

## from ... Over the Wine
### Victor Daley

Very often when I'm drinking,
   Of the old days I am thinking,
Of the good old days when living was a joy,
   And each morning brought new pleasure,
   And each night brought dreams of treasure,
And I thank the lord that I was once a boy.

For not all the trains in motion,
   All the ships that sail the ocean
With their cargoes; all the money in the mart,
   Could purchase for an hour
   Such a treasure as the flower,
As the flower of Hope that blossomed in my heart.

Now I sit and smile and listen
   To my friends whose eyes still glisten
Though their beards are showing threads of silver-grey,
   As they talk of fame and glory,
   The old, old pathetic story,
While they drink "Good luck" to luck that keeps away.

And I hate the cant of striving,
   Slaving, planning and contriving,
Struggling onward for a paltry little prize.

*Oh, it fills my heart with sorrow*
*This mad grasping for Tomorrow,*
*While Today from gold to purple dusks and dies.*

*Very often when I'm drinking,*
*Of the old days I am thinking,*
*Of the good old days when living was a joy,*
*When I see folk marching dreary*
*To the tune of Miserere*
*Then I thank the Lord that I am still a boy.*

# The Reformation

# Introduction

Resolutions, reforms and changes. Here are stories of situations and events which mould lives and change circumstances. These changes of direction are all accomplished through a journey of some kind down the liquid avenue of alcohol.

Not all these stories have happy resolutions but all share the commonality of some sort of resolution or change in life which is due at least partly to alcohol.

Some merely make accurate observations about change and the nature of change. "The Pub that Lost its Licence", for example, will strike a chord with all of us who harbour memories of those warm and friendly drinking establishments of our youth. When I was a young man there was a different sort of pub on every corner in the CBD of Sydney. Different professions frequented different pubs and each had its own flavour.

In my college days a pub crawl started at the White Horse in King Street, Newtown, and progressed down Broadway and then along George Street to finish at the Ship Inn. To finish took a mighty effort, even when you were restricted to one side of the road. Faint hearts didn't last past Central Railway. Today I imagine it would be difficult to become inebriated doing a pub crawl along that route. The majority of those pubs, including the White Horse, no longer exist. Sydney has truly undergone a "reformation" of drinking establishments, as have most cities.

A parallel reformation has occurred in country towns. In many small towns licences have been transferred and towns have lost their only local pub. For all their faults these pubs were often the communal heart of the town and these smaller towns are now rather sad dying communities.

In larger towns pubs have lost their original character and their differences. Country pubs once catered to different clientele. The Commercial catered for travelling salesmen and businessmen, the Railway, close to the station, catered for train travellers and railwaymen. The Royal, Empire or Imperial were frequented by graziers and loyalists while the Australian was often the chosen haunt of shearers and "Labor Men". Different pubs supported different football codes and sports and each had its own unique character for all these reasons. Today these differences are mostly gone, replaced by generic bars and gaming rooms.

Even in smaller "two pub" towns, like Weelabarabak, the differences between the town's "good pub" and the town's "other pub" or "bloodhouse" were marked and obvious. I have tried to give an honest but affectionate account of one town's "other pub" in "The Day the Pub Didn't Burn Down". It was an old bush maxim that a perfect town always had to have two pubs, the one you drank at and the "other pub" where you went when you were barred from the good pub.

Of course some stories here deal with attempts at personal reform, both successful and unsuccessful. "Daniel's Reform" is a delightful story from the *Bulletin's* heyday which looks, with amusing irony, at two successful "reforms".

The classic story of reformed lives is Henry Lawson's "The Story of 'Gentleman-Once'". Here Lawson examines the whole business of reform and its associated difficulties. This story is very interesting historically as it is the best explanantion I have ever read of the phenomenon of the "remittance man" which played such a big part in Australia's social and cultural history in the late nineteenth century.

Marcus Clarke's story, "On Teetotalism", was quite a delightful surprise to me when I first read through it. It reads as very modern satire and the humour is almost zany and not unlike that of Lennie Lower, who also appears here with a short piece about the need to reform Christmas.

Perhaps my favourite piece here is "The Drunken Kangaroo". I find Kenneth Cook's descriptions of small town life very accurate to my own memories. Anyone who has experienced the delicate nature of dealing with small communities will find special amusement in the local sergeant's futile attempts to deal with the complications arising from the behaviour of a neighbour's alcoholic marsupial. The resulting comic attempts to somehow reform the creature provide wonderful reading.

And, when you can't reform your fellows … well then you must do that especially Australian thing and accept them for what they are. This is really the essence of Lawson's other story in this section, "Macquarie's Mate". Apart from being a wonderful character piece and an amusing tale with a twist or two, "Macquarie's Mate" demonstrates Lawson's ability to accurately portray the mood and conversation of men in a pub, something he spent a lifetime researching.

According to Lawson, who once again gets the final word, the rules of mateship not only meant non-judgmental acceptance of a man's condition and circumstances, reformed or not, but also unconditional assistance:

*Now this is the creed from the Book of the Bush,*
*Should be simple and plain to a dunce:*
*"If a man's in a fix you must send round the hat,*
*Were he gaol-bird or gentleman once."*

> "I have very poor and unhappy brains for drinking: I could well wish
> courtesy would invent some other custom of entertainment."

SHAKESPEARE, 1603, OTHELLO II:I

# Daniel's Reform
## J. Evison

Young Daniel wasted his substance in riotous living.

He was of negative virtue and salesman in a wholesale Sydney house until he won 2000 pound over the Melbourne Cup.

Whereon he explained to the boss, with superfluity of adjective, that boss and business could go to, blazes. Then Daniel went out and bought an oppressively refulgent sulky, silver-plated harness, white reins and a trotting mare he hadn't nerve to drive when quite sober, and which dotted him like milestones over the roads on his head when he wasn't, which was frequently. He lived at the rate of pounds an hour, patronised fighting men, betted at races, and, temporarily, by encouragement of Satan, won more money.

Naturally, the day came when he paraded the Domain with straws in his hair, blue death-adders in his bulged boots, and his otherwise void pockets stuffed with old-gold tarantulas. He recovered. Some Samaritan who had himself trodden the whisky-tangled Via Dolorosa gave him a suit of clothes, and Daniel, despite his infelix reputation, got a billet. For months he lived on the smell of an oil-rag, saving money and reputation. Then his jamboree was very regal. He awoke therefrom to the knowledge that Sydney was played-out for Daniel. He did not arise and go unto his father, who was a struggling cocky, walnut-faced, and as destitute of imagination as a Biblical lore. Had Daniel essayed the role of Prodigal Son, the old man would have fallen on his neck with a fence rail or bitten him. In Melbourne, however, resided a brother of Daniel's mother, Uriah Tregea, merchant, prosperous, married into Toorak and money, austerely respectable. This uncle, whom he had not seen for years, he determined to treat to the felicity of a prodigal nephew. Precisely how Daniel got to Melbourne he never knew, but he arrived, stone broke.

It was Sunday morning, and the Sabbath bells were ringing when Daniel sighted his uncle's villa. The prim ornateness of that residence discomposed him. "Bloomin' high-toned!" he muttered. He would temporise with fate. He picked a blade of grass to ruminate upon, sought the shade of a spreading elm, propped a zinc fence with his back, and watched Uncle Uriah's garden gate. Anon it opened and the lady from Toorak, a perfumed haze of laces, ribbons and flowers, floated out in command of a very small boy suffering from Sunday clothes. Mr Tregea followed.

Uncle Uriah, from the crown of his tall, shiny hat to the sole of his immaculate boots, was the apotheosis of modern male Christianity burnished for church parade. In his coat a choice gardenia bloomed; under his arm a gold-headed cane; on his hands, and this spectacle greatly depressed Daniel, faultless, tender-hued kid gloves. A well-looking, well-knit, highly-coloured dark man with penetrative eyes, a large, richly gilt church service, and a cold manner.

Daniel's boots were burst, his linen more than doubtful, the heels of his trousers deep-gnawed by Sydney pavements; the mire of travel and the stubble of an incoherent beard encrusted him; his hand shook. But he had a piece of soiled blue ribbon, emblem of a whiskyless life, in his buttonhole. He detached himself from the fence and slouched forward.

"Speak to you, 'f please!"

The lady swept him with the far-away gaze with which haughty Toorak surveys without seeing Little Bourke Street. Uncle Uriah halted.

He put his fingers into the pocket of his splendid waistcoat, extracting a shilling.

"Don't fatigue yourself to talk. Your poor old father is dying in Ballarat; you want to wire him your forgiveness, but they have no money! Take this shilling. They charge threepence each for your sort of telegrams, long ones, at the office down that street. You enter at the front door, *not* at the jug and bottle department."

It was a great temptation, four beers! Four long, long beers! Ah!

"But I'm, I'm your nephew, I'm Daniel Pye!"

Uncle Uriah remained calm. He did not bring forth the best robe. He did not order fatted veal for dinner.

"Well?"

"I thought, uncle, perhaps …"

"Spare yourself the exertion of detail. When did you last wash?"

"I … I …"

"Precisely. See that lady?"

"Yes."

"Your aunt! She objects to young Australia ungroomed and perfumed with colonial beer — bad beer, I should judge by the odour. Prejudice, doubtless; still — her way. Come with me."

He led the young man down a grass-grown side street to the door of a rural pub. The landlord stood without, praying that he might do a good Sabbath trade, that being illegal, and consequently universal.

"Come inside, Potts."

Potts followed, widely smiling.

"This young man will stay here. He wants — well, he wants curry-combing first, then a warm bath, a shave, and clean linen. Please have him seen to. After he's scoured, give him one big drink, another in the afternoon, and one at night, no more."

"But I'm a teetotaller, uncle."

Mr Tregea languidly waved his gloved hand. "See he attends my office, sharp ten to-morrow, will you, Potts?"

As Uncle Uriah and Potts went out Daniel voiced acute discontent:

"You might make it *four* drinks, I think, uncle!"

When Mr Potts returned Daniel said, haughtily, "Bring in a bottle of whisky, boss."

"No, you don't! Come and have that there bath."

Next morning Potts, acting under instructions, conveyed Daniel into Melbourne for refittal. An (externally) amended Daniel, with much shirt-collar, a white waistcoat, horticulture in his coat, and a quavering jauntiness of demeanour, waited upon Mr Tregea.

"Permit me to do the talking," said the latter. "I am in possession of your interesting biography. You have done everything but steal.

"You have no morals; you can work, by spasms. Sick of industry, you revel in long beers and debauchery. I'm going to reform you, going to make you morally sweet and clean, or expend you in the effort. You will come into this office. You will live near me so that I can personally supervise your reformation. If you as much as smell liquor I propose to make you very sorry. When you have worn off the odour of dissipation I will introduce you to your aunt. The example of virtuous and pure-minded people may redeem even you. The manager will now show you your work. That will do."

The old hands in uncle Tregea's business thrust the tongue of derision into the cheek of contempt at Daniel. But not for long. He worked early and late. In three months he was teaching the boss salesman how to sell. As he grew in grace he was introduced to his aunt, who accepted him with toleration, as another development of her husband's eccentricity. The atmosphere of uncle Tregea's house was surcharged with gentility, so much so that Daniel, who had an undistinguished perspicacity, sometimes fancied that his uncle was a trifle bored by the Toorakian culture which fenced him in by night as by day.

Occasionally, when he and Daniel were alone, uncle Uriah would consume a bottle of what the prodigal nephew contemptuously termed "soft tack", with a gentle sigh, but whether a sigh of enjoyment or as a tribute to the absence of whisky, Mrs Tregea totally tabooed alcohol and tobacco, owing to their innate vulgarity, Daniel could not determine.

Sometimes his uncle would express a tempered satisfaction with Daniel's progress towards virtue. "Isn't the consciousness of living cleanly and morally, or being associated with good people who neither smoke, drink, nor swear, but who have tone and culture, infinitely nobler and more satisfying than wallowing in drink and the rest?"

Daniel agreed, without torrid enthusiasm. He had acquired, however, a deep veneration for his uncle, the more profound because he could not understand how any man, let alone one with money, could lead so immaculate a life. Daniel almost yawned himself into tears when he thought of that uncoloured existence, that Sahara of respectability, without a single oasis of razzle-dazzle. But he regarded uncle Uriah as a model man, while admitting to himself that "uncle isn't very fly".

"How long have you been with me?"

"More'n six months, uncle."

"And totally abstained all the time?"

"Abstained! Never even sniffed a cork, uncle."

"Think you're reformed?"

"*Certain*, wouldn't go on a bend now for any money."

"You excruciating young ass. Don't you see you're not *resisting* temptation, but only running away from it?"

"How?"

"You must face, touch and taste drink, and beat it, not let it beat you."

"Oh!" said Daniel, with a clear glint in his dark eyes.

"Yes, I've thought this out, and, though I hate to do it, I mean to fly round — that's what you call it, fly round, with you of a night. You shall take me to just the sort of places you used to frequent, hotels, billiard rooms, races, and low resorts, I presume. And you shall learn to take your liquor and to face these vulgar excitements without descending to brute level. When you can do that you'll be really reformed."

"Yes!" said Daniel, solemnly, with a gentle smacking of his lips. He added, "But, aunt!"

"Well, I loathe deceit, but in this case the end sanctifies the means. Your aunt thinks we have work that will keep us, and for many weeks, late at the office of a night."

"Ah-h-h!"

"Suppose you've saved money, eh?" enquired Uncle Uriah one night after they had dined copiously in town.

"Saved all my screw, uncle, except what I pay for board."

"Very good; we play billiards tonight — for money. I abhor gambling, and I shall play solely in your interest."

"This is going to be a very soft thing for Daniel," chuckled the prodigal. "Don't suppose uncle can play for sour apples."

Yet, when Daniel counted the cost, he whistled dubiously. "If uncle was anybody else, I should place him as a swagger billiard sharp!" he sadly soliloquised.

For long, the young man relaxed himself with noble moderation. One night, however, as they were proceeding towards the station, en route for home, he exhibited symptoms of quicksilver poisoning — the mercury apparently coursing about his system. His legs would suddenly go limp, or his spine bulge, or his head start wobbling like an articulated porcelain nodding Chinese mandarin. Contemporaneously, his manner visibly swelled, acquiring a compativeness utterly foreign to his normal deference towards his uncle.

"Made a beast of yourself, I see!"

"Washthatushayuncl'?"

"I remarked you had turned to your wallow, like any other hog!"

"Lookereuncle, … wontletshu … n'anyother … mansh talkmeliketharsh. I disown you — dishown you! Put up your propsh — goin' to biff you uncle!"

And the wretched prodigal actually smote his benevolent relative somewhere about the third waistcoat-button — smote him scientifically and hard. The ensuing scene was swift and distressing. Uncle Uriah threw out his left, then swung his right in a *degage* but painful manner. Result, Daniel on his back in the gutter, contemplating the cerulean dome of heaven with one partially open eye, the other being closed utterly, pending repairs. Then his uncle picked him up with one hand, pitched him into a cab, and sat on him.

Daniel, subsequently cogitating, never quite reconciled his uncle's rapid right with his uncle's unblemished respectability and innocence of worldly affairs. "Wonder where he learned that trick! S'pose that's a cultured, pure-minded right of uncle's. It's terribly sudden, though," he reflected.

The prodigal went into retreat to mend. In a fortnight, with misgivings, he reported himself to his uncle. "Go to your work. I said I'd reform you, and, by high heaven, I will!"

Daniel, pondering all these things in his heart, felt that ignoble advantage had been taken of his youth and ill-regulated thirst. He related his afflictions to the present writer. "You see," he said, "it's all very fine for uncle, who's genteel and strong-minded; he sips about two drinks, I expect, while I'm filling myself up, then he gives me peculiar goss for not having self-control. I'd like to know who'd have self-control when uncle keeps saying, 'Fill the gentleman's glass again, please, miss!'"

"Fill *him* up," I suggested.

"Strike me, I will!"

I learned later that the ingenuous youth had poured, at his own expense, which was contrary to his principles — large quantities of whisky into Mr Tregea while slyly throwing his own liquor away. When they adjourned Uncle Uriah, frigid as the Antarctic

Pole, spoke to Daniel seriously and at length, regarding the "brutal avidity" with which the younger man consumed intoxicants. "You don't drink your liquor, you eat it, sir! You make me shudder to see you. But I'll reform you yet!"

Daniel was very disheartened.

"And there's billiards," he sighed to me; "I never smell a single game. Uncle flukes somethin' sickenin', but he always gets there. He owns he flukes. He's won a pot of money off me."

"Try him at euchre, Daniel."

Which Daniel did, stacking the cards frightfully. Mr Tregea's soul revolted against cards. He said so. But he sacrificed himself in the cause of reform, and broke poor Daniel up badly at the new pastime.

About this time the latter frequently woke up, suffering, in the morning, with a fancy that his uncle had been badly tangled the previous evening, and that he (Daniel) had piloted, the blind leading the blinder, him home. But when later, he beheld uncle, spick, clear-eyed, and garbed more gloriously than Solomon, and heard uncle deplore his (Daniel's) easy fall to temptation, the latter knew his fancy for the fabric of a dream.

A crisis in the prodigal's reformation approached. They were waiting one afternoon at a suburban station for a Melbourne train, Daniel in a mental condition favourable to sarcasm. A huge butcher's slaughterman pushed against him rudely, and Daniel explained to the man that he would find the pig-trucks lower down on to the permanent way. There were brief proceedings, and a partially slaughtered slaughterman was carried away to be sewn up and to apply the familiar bullock to his bulged eyes, while the stationmaster and a guard were appraising personal injuries resultant on injudicious interference.

Two mornings after, Mr Tregea handed Daniel an official-looking letter.

"This came to my house; kindly have your correspondence directed to your own residence."

Daniel read and turned *eau-de-nil* tint.

A lofty railway official wrote that legal proceedings for desperate assaults and language would be taken against Daniel Pye. Before framing the very serious charges, the official would be willing to hear anything which would be urged in extenuation.

Daniel, trembling, handed his uncle the letter. "Just so!" said Uncle Uriah. "Taken into the bosom of my family, afforded every example of rectitude and virtue, you disgrace me and pollute my home by your loathsome appetites and murderous violence."

"But what did I do, uncle? Wish I may die 'f I know. I clean forget everything. If I was accused of murder I couldn't deny it."

"That's about what it is. You murderously assaulted a butcher. Certainly he hit you first; but you struck the railway people, and your language made my blood run cold."

"How did they know my name, though?"

"I … I gave them your card, to prevent you being locked up."

"But I never carry cards when … when I'm out for pleasure."

"No? Well, I happened to have one of your cards in my pocket."

"Say, uncle!"

"Well?"

"I'll clear for Tasmania."

"You won't. You'll go and see this railway officer, tell him the truth, and beg for mercy. If you as much as mention me in the matter I will myself compel the railway people to prosecute you."

Daniel saw the official. Dressed in deepest mourning, wearing a racking cough and his left arm in splints, he wept copiously into a large cambric handkerchief and explained to the august presence that he was an orphan, also that, previous to the day of his misfortune he had been in bed for six months (consumption, he feared). He had been induced (by a bad companion) to go to the races, and had taken one, only one, glass of spirits, the first he had ever tasted in his life. It was wrong to do so. Wrong to go to races. He had a billet to go to, tomorrow, in a bank; all his poor orphaned little brothers and sisters were solely dependent upon him; he was their breadwinner; a public scandal would, of course ruin him and them. Perhaps the gentleman had sons of his own?

He had, and was quite touched by Daniel's pathos and penitence. He lectured Daniel gravely (then Daniel put away his pocket handkerchief); he could not understand how a person of Daniel's physique could have inflicted such terrible punishment on that butcher (Daniel couldn't understand it either); however, the butcher was the aggressor; he had hit Daniel's companion (Daniel did not correct the statement); but there were the assaults on the railway servants, serious offences!

Eventually the official consented to forego prosecution, which would certainly entail imprisonment, on condition Daniel paid five pounds to Melbourne Hospital and apologised to the wounded railway men.

Daniel went straight out and buttonholed the stationmaster, and grovelled before him for having polluted his station by shedding the gore of a butcher thereon, and having incidentally damaged the stationmaster.

The latter stared very hard, and simply said. "You must be off your chump, I think." He probably said more than that, but no artifice ever succeeded in making Daniel repeat what he then heard.

"It's this way," said Daniel to me next day; "I shall never taste again, not as long as poor uncle wants me with him. You see, I've only just dodged Pentridge this twist. Next time it'll be murder, and I shall swing, certain, I don't know what I do, when I'm full. I thought I was pretty fly, but I'm a mug, I am. I'm not in it with high-tone and culture. Uncle's a good man; he's been good to me; but, but Uncle's cunnin', he is; I don't suppose there's a cunnin'er man in Victoria than uncle Uriah! He took me to reform me. Well, he has!"

"What d'ye mean?" I asked.

"Never mind — I know. No more liquor, no more sprees for Daniel; he's reformed, Daniel is."

Said Mr Tregea to me, "I think I've made a job of that youngster. I've reformed him, I said I would. There was more vanity than vice in him. He was touchingly inexperienced."

"Do you know," I remarked, "I think Daniel is under the impression, he's been talking to the stationmaster, that it was *you* who smashed the butcher and *you* who damaged the railway people and used lurid language. Was it?"

"My dear sir," he replied, "you must have taken leave of your senses. *Me*! Why, just Heaven, they elected me churchwarden only yesterday."

# Macquarie's Mate
## Henry Lawson

The chaps in the bar of Stiffner's Shanty were talking about Macquarie, an absent shearer who seemed, from their conversation, to be better known than liked.

"I ain't seen Macquarie for ever so long," remarked Box-o'-Tricks, after a pause. "Wonder where he could 'a' got to?"

"Gaol, p'r'aps — or hell," growled Barcoo. "He ain't much loss, any road."

"My oath, yer right, Barcoo!" interposed "Sally" Thompson. "But, now I come to think of it, old Awful Example there was a mate of his one time. Bless'd if the old soaker ain't comin' to life again!"

A shaky, rag-and-dirt-covered framework of a big man rose uncertainly from a corner of the room, and, staggering forward, brushed the staring thatch back from his forehead with one hand, reached blindly for the edge of the bar with the other, and drooped heavily.

"Well, Awful Example," demanded the shanty keeper. "What's up with you now?"

The drunkard lifted his head and glared wildly round with bloodshot eyes.

"Don't you — don't you talk about him. *Drop it*, I say! *Drop* it!"

"What the devil's the mater with you now, anyway?" growled the barman. "Got 'em again? Hey?"

"Don't you … don't you talk about Macquarie! He's mate of mine! Here! Gimme a drink!"

"Well, what if he is a mate of yours?" sneered Barcoo. "It don't reflec' much credit on you, nor him neither."

The logic contained in the last three words was unanswerable, and Awful Example was still fairly reasonable, even when rum oozed out of him at every pore. He gripped the edge of the bar with both hands, let his ruined head fall forward until it was on a level with his temporarily rigid arms, and stared blindly at the dirty floor; then he straightened himself up, still keeping his hold on the bar.

"Some of you chaps," he said huskily; "*one* of you chaps, in this bar today, called Macquarie a scoundrel, and a loafer, and a blackguard and … and a sneak, and a liar."

"Well, what if we did?" said Barcoo defiantly. "He's all that, and a cheat into the bargain. And now, what are you going to do about it?"

The old man swung sideways to the bar, rested his elbow on it and his head on his hand.

"Macquarie wasn't a sneak and he wasn't a liar," he said in a quiet, tired tone; "and Macquarie wasn't a cheat!"

"Well, old man, you needn't get your rag out about it," said Sally Thompson, soothingly. "P'r'aps we was a bit too hard on him; and it isn't altogether right, chaps, considerin' he's not here. But then, you know, Awful, he might have acted straight to you that was his mate. The meanest blank — if he is a man at all — will do that."

"Oh, to blazes with the old sot!" shouted Barcoo. "I gave my opinion about Macquarie and, what's more, I'll stand to it."

"I've got … I've got a point for the defence," the old man went on, without heeding the interruptions. "I've got a point or two for the defence."

"Well, let's have it," said Stiffner.

"In the first place … in the first place, Macquarie never talked about no man behind his back."

There was an uneasy movement and a painful silence. Barcoo reached for his drink and drank it slowly; he needed time to think. Box-o'-Tricks studied his boots, Sally Thompson looked out at the weather, the shanty keeper wiped the top of the bar very hard and the rest shifted round and "s'posed they'd try a game er cards".

Barcoo set his glass down very softly, pocketed his hands deeply and defiantly, and said: "Well, what of that? Macquarie was as strong as a bull, and the greatest bully on the river into the bargain. He could call a man a liar to his face — and smash his face afterwards. And he did it often, too, and with smaller men than himself."

There was a breath of relief in the bar.

"Do you want to make out that I'm talking about a man behind his back?" continued Barcoo threateningly to Awful Example. "You'd best take care, old man."

"Macquarie wasn't a coward," remonstrated the drunkard softly, but in an injured tone.

"What's up with you, anyway?" yelled the publican. "What yer growlin' at? D'ye want a row? Get out if yer can't be agreeable!"

The boozer swung his back to the bar, hooked himself on by his elbows and looked vacantly out of the door.

"I've got — another point of defence," he muttered. "It's always best, it's always best to keep the last point till, till the last."

"Oh, Lord! Well, out with it! *Out with it!*"

"*Macquarie's dead!* That … that's what it is!"

Everyone moved uneasily: Sally Thompson turned the other side to the bar, crossed one leg behind the other, and looked down over his hip at the sole and heel of his elastic-side — the barman rinsed the glasses vigorously, Longbone shuffled and dealt on the top of a cask, and some of the others gathered round him and got interested. Barcoo thought he heard his horse breaking away, and went out to see to it, followed by Box-o'-Tricks and a couple more who thought that it might be one of their horses.

Someone, a tall, gaunt, determined-looking bushman, with square features and haggard grey eyes, had ridden in unnoticed through the scrub to the back of the shanty and dismounted by the window.

When Barcoo and the others re-entered the bar it soon became evident that Sally Thompson had been thinking, for presently he came to the general rescue as follows: "There's a blessed lot of tommy rot about dead people in this world, a lot of damned old woman nonsense. There's more sympathy wasted over dead and rotten skunks than there is justice done to straight, honest livin' chaps. I don't b'lieve in this gory sentiment about the dead at the expense of the living. I b'lieve in justice for the livin' — and the dead too, for that matter — but justice for the livin'. Macquarie was a bad egg, and it don't alter the case if he was dead a thousand times."

There was another breath of relief in the bar, and presently somebody said: "Yer right, Sally!"

"Good for you, Sally, old man!" cried Box-o'-Tricks, taking it up. "An', besides, I don't b'lieve Macquarie is dead at all. He's always dyin' or being reported dead, and then turnin' up again. Where did you hear about it, Awful?"

The Example ruefully rubbed a corner of his roof with the palm of his hand. "There's … there's a lot in what you say, Sally Thompson," he admitted slowly, totally ignoring Box-o'-Tricks. "But … but …"

"Oh, we've had enough of the old fool," yelled Barcoo. "Macquarie was a spieler, and any man that 'ud be his mate ain't much better."

"Here, take a drink and dry up, yer old hass!" said the man behind the bar, pushing a bottle and glass towards the drunkard. "D'ye want a row?"

The old man took the bottle and glass in his shaking hands and painfully poured out a drink.

"There's a lot in what Sally Thompson says," he went on, obstinately, "but, but," he added in a strained tone, "there's another point that I near forgot, and none of you seemed to think of it — not even Sally Thompson nor … nor Box-o'-Tricks there."

Stiffner turned his back, and Barcoo spat viciously and impatiently.

"Yes," drivelled the drunkard, "I've got another point for … for the defence … of my mate, Macquarie …"

"Oh, out with it! Spit it out, for God's sake, or you'll bust!" roared Stiffner. "What the blazes is it?"

"His *mate's alive!*" yelled the old man. "Macquarie's mate's alive! That's what it is!"

He reeled back from the bar, dashed his glass and hat to the boards, gave his pants a hitch by the waistband that almost lifted him off his feet and tore at his shirtsleeves.

"Make a ring boys," he shouted. "His mate's alive! Put up your hands, Barcoo! By God, his mate's alive!"

Someone had turned his horse loose at the rear and had been standing by the back door for the last five minutes. Now he slipped quietly in.

"Keep the old fool off, or he'll get hurt," snarled Barcoo.

Stiffner jumped the counter. There were loud, hurried words of remonstrance, then some stump-splitting oaths and a scuffle, consequent upon an attempt to chuck the old man out. Then a crash. Stiffner and Box-o'-Tricks were down, two others were holding Barcoo back and someone had pinned Awful Example by the shoulders from behind.

"Let me go!" he yelled, too blind with passion to notice the movements of surprise among the men before him. "Let me go! I'll smash … any man … that … that says a word again' a mate of mine behind his back. Barcoo, I'll have your blood! Let me go! I'll … I'll … Who's holdin' me? You … you …"

"It's Macquarie, old mate!" said a quiet voice.

Barcoo thought he heard his horse again, and went out in a hurry. Perhaps he thought that the horse would get impatient and break loose if he left it any longer, for he jumped into the saddle and rode off.

> *"Abstinence is as easy to me, as temperance would be difficult."*
>
> DR SAMUEL JOHNSON, 1760

# On Teetotalism
## Marcus Clarke

I am not a teetotaller, at least, not now. I used to be, but my constitution is not strong, and I could not stand the dissipation.

Cordials, as a general rule, are worse than liquor; there is more brandy in them. A teetotaller who has been drinking Balm of Gilead is a terrible sight, more especially when he sits in the gutter and holds the lamp-posts steady. I made a calculation once, and found that no teetotaller could possibly live through more than ten years of *cordiality*. It destroys the coats of their stomachs. My stomach used to go about in its shirtsleeves habitually, and that is how I got cold in my inside.

I used to be a dreadful fellow, nearly as bad as the drunkards in the storybook. I have been drunk for a year and a half at a stretch. It was natural for me to drink. When I was about three days and a half old, I saw my nurse hide a brandy bottle away in a cupboard that she couldn't get at afterwards. I never said anything about it then, but as soon as I could walk, I got the keys and drank that brandy.

I didn't get better as I grew older; quite the contrary. I used to drink so that the publicans, when they went out of business, used to sell *me* among the valuable fixtures. A great many people tried to convert me. The teetotal lecturers used to lay bets on it with the ungodly, and the ungodly won.

They used to use all sorts of arguments with me. One gentleman said that I was a miserable creature, and that if he had the keys of heaven he would let me in. I said that it would be a lucky thing for him if I had the keys of the other place, because then I could let him out. He wasn't a bad fellow, though, for he used to preach in a room next to the kitchen and he always stopped when he heard the ham fizzing. He was a religious man, but smart.

There was another man who tackled me regularly, laid himself alongside, in sailor phrase, but he gave in, too, after about three square feet of brown brandy. It was all very well preaching, but during the five years of my converting process no teetotal lecturer ever saw me intoxicated, for before I was three sheets in the wind he was just blind drunk.

I was converted in a strange way at last. It was old Joe's pork sausage that converted me. Old Joe, Bullocky Joe, we used to call him, lived on the Glenelg, and kept a small public house at the Ford. Joe had a theory that public houses came naturally alongside rivers, because of the convenience for watering grog. He was a good-tempered, honest fellow, with one eye, and had been transported for killing his mother with a pole-axe. Joe was very fond of animals, especially cats, and made the best pork sausages I ever ate. Joe was a friend of mine. When Joe was tried for horse stealing, he had such confidence in me that he sent for me all the way from the Darling to swear an alibi, which I did successfully. After trial, he said, with tears in his eyes, "God bless you, old fellow; you are the hardest swearer of any man I ever met, and you shall have the run of your teeth in my house till you die."

Joe was a man of his word, but I think that when he saw the way I used to coil away his sausages, he regretted his outburst of manly emotion. Ah! Why, many and many a time have I gone away from Joe's with twelve helpings of sausages under the brass cricketer that kept my belt from bursting.

One day, though, a teetotal lecturer came to the Ford and put up at Joe's. Joe had bought an old sheepdog from a swagman that morning, and we had sausages for supper. I ate a pretty meal, but the lecturer, Mr Josiah J. Smawkins, he called himself — beat me into stale oysters at it. He was like a whirlpool to a kitchen sink, compared to me. The way he lowered down Joe's sausages was beautiful yet terrible, like a thunderstorm. Strive my hardest, but it was no use. I couldn't beat him, so I gave up.

Well, he preached that night powerfully, sir, started all the nails in the roof, and then he lowered down more sausages, and drank ginger beer until I thought he would blow his head off.

In the morning he came down to breakfast looking solemn; and Joe says, "I hope you've had a good night, Mr. Smawkins."

"Well," says Mr. Smawkins, "I have not; I had dreams, sir."

"Oh, indeed, sir," says Joe, "and what did you dream?"

"I dreamt a most extraordinary dream. I never had such a dream before."

"Indeed!" said I, with my mouth full.

"Yes," said Mr. Smawkins. "I dreamed that I was lying on the grass under a she-oak tree, with a mob of sheep feeding in front of me, when some one called out, 'Hey, Jock, ye damned villun, get away forrard,' and then, sir, I got upon my hands and knees, and went off after the sheep; and when I'd got 'em all together, the same voice cried. 'Come in ahint, yer black scroondrel; come in ahint or I'll cut the liver out of yer.' And this went on all night, sir, I was always 'going forward', and 'rounding up', and 'coming in ahint'; and I'm tired this morning as if I had been twenty miles."

Joe began to laugh, but I caught sight of a black-and-tan hide hanging up outside the pantry door, and turned deathly sick. The unsuspecting Smawkins finished "Jock", and rose to go. As his buggy, a sort of perambulating invalid go-kart slung upon wheels, drawn by a horse roughly sketched in bone, came round to the door, I grasped the hand of the holy man, and said: "Excuse me, sir, but can all teetotallers eat like you?"

"All," said he, with a calm smile; and, waving his hand, he leapt into his buggy, the horse broke into full walk, and in less than half-an-hour the equipage was lost in sight.

I became a teetotaller at once, and would be so still, but for the miserable quality of my constitution. As Mr Burnett said to me long ago, "You will never be one of us. You have ruined your constitution by early temperance."

> "'Tis not the drinking that is to be blamed, but the excess."
>
> JOHN SELDEN, 1689

# The Drunken Kangaroo
## Kenneth Cook

My deep fear of all Australian animals probably stems from my childhood association with an alcoholic kangaroo.

My father was a policeman and for a time was stationed at Walgett in northern New South Wales. He, my mother and I found ourselves living next door to an old man who kept as a pet a huge red kangaroo.

The old man's name was Benny and he called his kangaroo Les after a famous boxer. Benny was a fuzzy-haired, sparrow-like man with a sweet disposition. Les was almost two metres of muscle and malice. I never saw why Benny was so fond of him.

Les lived in Benny's backyard. It was surrounded by a tall paling fence which he simply hopped over when he wanted to get out. He wanted to get out at least six times a day, and poor old Benny spent most of his life trying to persuade Les to come home. Benny used to get badly bruised in these encounters because the roo had a habit of hitting him with his forepaws, kicking him with his hind legs or whacking him with his tail when Benny tried to catch him.

Sometimes Benny tried to take Les for walks on a lead, and it was a sad sight to see that nice man being dragged through the main street of Walgett by a massive marsupial given to punching, kicking or whacking him with great frequency.

People often advised Benny to turn Les loose, or, better still, to convert him into dog's meat, but Benny would protest that he loved the animal and, contrary to all the evidence, the animal loved him.

At that stage, Les was no problem to anybody else in Walgett and if Benny wanted to maintain an unusual association with a kangaroo, that was his business. Nobody interfered.

My father and I became quite friendly with Benny and often used to help him catch Les and bring him home. It was an exciting business, and I used to enjoy it, particularly as Les never punched, kicked or whacked anybody but Benny.

But then Les took to drink and became a public menace.

There was a brewery in Walgett in those days, and every Wednesday the hops mash was strained off the brew and dumped at the rear of the premises in a large pond.

Les discovered this on one of his jaunts, tasted it and found he loved the beery, sloppy mess. He ate and ate until he fell down in an alcoholic stupor.

Benny learned of this when a messenger from the brewery called to tell him that his bloody kangaroo had dropped dead in the rear of the brewery premises and would he please get the corpse out of there immediately.

Poor old Benny was distraught, and enlisted my father and me to help him. The three of us trooped down to the brewery and found Les not dead, but very, very unconscious.

"He's mortal bad," keened Benny in his squeaky old voice.

"No, he's not," said my father, eyeing the great pool of hops mash and noting that the same stuff was liberally splattered over the kangaroo's brutish face. "He's rotten drunk."

Benny pleaded with us to help get Les home. My father was a big man, and strong, and I wasn't bad for my age. Benny wasn't much use. The three of us grabbed Les by the tail and tried to drag him home. But half a tonne of comatose kangaroo is hard to drag and we finally had to go and get a draughthorse to do the job. We rolled Les onto a gate and the draughthorse dragged him the half kilometre or so to Benny's backyard.

We left Benny covering Les with a blanket and pressing wet towels to his forehead, if kangaroos can be said to have foreheads.

I was there the next morning when Les finally woke up. Benny was squatting next to him, holding his right paw, as he had apparently been doing all night. Les opened one eye with extreme care. It was very bloodshot. He shut it quickly. There was a long pause, during which Benny clucked and tutted sympathetically, and then the kangaroo opened both bloodshot eyes. I swear he winced.

My memory may be playing me false, but I am convinced that at this point Les very slowly and clumsily scrambled to his feet and leaned against the paling fence, holding both front paws to his head. He groaned. Kangaroos do groan.

Benny went rushing off to get a bucket of water and Les drank the lot without pausing for breath, which is normally a very difficult thing for a kangaroo to do.

The water seemed to help him a lot. He stood looking reflectively into the empty bucket. Then suddenly he leaped straight over the paling fence and went bolting down the street towards the brewery.

"After him!" squeaked Benny, flung open the gate and went hobbling after the kangaroo as fast as a man of eighty or so can hobble, which is not very fast.

I ran ahead of him and managed to keep Les in sight. He made straight for the brewery, leaped the two-strand wire fence around the rear of the building, flung himself into the hops mash and began sucking the stuff up as though his life depended on it. He probably felt that it did.

I stood helplessly at the edge of the pond, watching the huge kangaroo, waist-deep in hops mash, plunging his head again and again into the yeasty mess, eating, imbibing, inhaling the whole highly alcoholic mixture. I later realised that I was witnessing a classic case of instant alcoholic addiction.

Benny came panting up and nearly burst into tears when he saw what was happening.

"Come out of it, Les, you naughty kangaroo," he cried, "you'll make yourself sick as a dog." Les took no notice whatsoever.

"Go and get your father, boy," squeaked Benny. I shot back home and told my father what was happening. A kindly man, he stroked his beard and thought for a moment.

"He's actually in the pond this time?"

"Yes."

"So if he takes in enough of the stuff, he'll probably pass out and drown?"

"Yes, I suppose so."

"Might be the best possible solution," said my father.

But I was young and fond of Benny. I pleaded with my father to come to the rescue. He eventually collected a rope and the draught horse and we returned to the brewery.

Quite a crowd had gathered by then. Old Benny was literally in tears as he pleaded with Les to pull himself together and give up the drink. Les determinedly continued to try and absorb enough of the hops mash to render himself insensible.

My father made a lassoo out of the rope, threw it over Les's chest and tied the other end around the neck of the draughthorse. Les was hauled from the pond kicking and grunting and desperately trying to swallow a few more mouthfuls.

As soon as he was on dry land, dripping hops mash, he turned ugly. This was no comatose, alcohol-sodden marsupial: this was a fighting drunk kangaroo. He leaped at my father, grunting angrily, and knocked him down with one mighty kick. Then he turned on the crowd, who ran away shrieking. Les went after them but was brought up short by the rope around his chest. He turned and went for the draughthorse. The draughthorse looked at him sourly and kicked him in the stomach. Les stood for a moment, gasping, and Benny rushed in and threw his arms around the beast. Les drew back his left paw, struck and knocked Benny flat on his back.

My father had recovered a little by then but was still obviously dazed. He drew his revolver and advanced on Les, shouting, "Surrender in the name of the king!"

Les just stood there, grunting furiously.

"Surrender in the king's name," repeated my father, pointing his revolver, "or I'll blow your bloody head off!"

Benny was on his feet now and he flung himself between my father and Les. The conversation became inconsequential.

"You can't shoot a kangaroo," said Benny.

"Yes, I can," said my father. "I have, often."

"But this is a civilised kangaroo," said Benny. "You can't shoot a civilised kangaroo without a charge."

"The charge is being drunk and disorderly," roared my father.

"But you don't shoot people for being drunk and disorderly," pleaded Benny.

"Kangaroos aren't people," said my father, who could never resist an argument.

"There you are," said Benny triumphantly. "That's exactly what I mean."

"Eh?" said my father.

Les, meanwhile, on a slack rope, had slipped back into the pond and was absorbing hops mash again.

"You wouldn't shoot my old mate, would you, man?" asked Benny piteously.

My father, whose head seemed to be clearing, began to see the funny side of the situation. He slipped his revolver back into its holster.

"All right," he said, "I'll tell you what we'll do. Let him guzzle on for a while. He'll get dopey, then we'll drag him out and toss him in the lockup until he's sober."

So that's what we did. Les went on tucking into the hops for about half an hour, then he started to sway, went cross-eyed and was about to collapse when my father began to lead away the draughthorse, to which Les was still attached.

"What are you doing with my kangaroo?" squeaked Benny.

"I told you," said my father. "I'm going to gaol him until he sobers up." He pulled out his handcuffs, preparatory to handcuffing Les's legs together, if you can handcuff legs.

"How long are you going to lock him up for?" asked Benny.

"Until I'm satisfied that he's no longer a public danger," said my father.

"But you can't do that without charging him," said Benny. "I'll have habeas corpus on you."

"Then I'll charge him," said my father desperately.

"With what?"

"Disturbing the peace, being drunk and disorderly, assault, resisting arrest, causing a public disturbance, I've got enough on your bloody kangaroo to keep him in gaol for life. Now stop making a fuss, or I'll shoot him dead for trying to escape."

"But he's not trying to escape," said Benny plaintively.

"What's that got to do with it?" asked my father.

"I'm going to get a lawyer," cried Benny and hobbled away purposefully.

While all this legal argument was going on, Les unobtrusively slipped out of the noose and went bounding drunkenly up the main street. He was far from being comatose; he was in an advanced state of delirium tremens.

The street was packed with horses and sulkies, drays, motor cars, shoppers, old ladies and small children.

Les was bounding higher and more wildly than any sober kangaroo possibly could. Emitting loud explosive grunts, he went over the head of a horse harnessed to a cart and kicked it on the nose as he passed. The horse whinnied, reared and bolted. Les blundered into a shop window and smashed it. Two old ladies had hysterics.

My father, revolver drawn again, went racing after the kangaroo, but his shooting was restricted by fear of killing too many innocent civilians. Les stunned an old gentleman with his tail, then did shocking damage to an expensive motor car with his rear claws.

My father got close enough for a safe shot, but missed (he was a rotten marksman) and blew out another shop window. Les leaped over four fat middle-aged ladies, three of whom fainted. My father tripped over one of them and accidentally shot the tyre of a motor bus. All the passengers started to scream. The main street of Walgett, for the first and probably last time, was like a Marx Bros movie.

Finally Les stopped in front of a pub, as though instinctively looking for more drink. My father caught up with him and loosed off four shots at point-blank range. They all missed and the pub window suffered irreparable damage. But Les's booze-soaked mind finally grasped the fact that he was in real danger. He turned and bolted out of town.

My father commandeered a car and went after him, still shooting, but soon lost him when Les turned off the road and went into the scrub.

Benny was disconsolate. "I loved that kangaroo," he told my father reproachfully, "and now you've frightened him right out of my life."

Privately my father thought he had done Benny a favour, but he was a soft-hearted policeman and he caught a young wallaby and gave it to the old man as a pet. "But for God's sake, keep it off the grog," he warned.

"Well, thank you," said Benny, wrapping his arms around the wallaby, "but it's a terrible thing to know I'll never see Les again."

This wasn't true. Les came into town every Wednesday night, after the new hops mash had been poured into the pond, got disgustingly drunk and cleared out before dawn.

Lots of people saw him, but he didn't do any more harm so nobody bothered about him.

He went on doing this for five years. Then the brewery closed down, there was no hops mash, and nothing more was seen of Les.

But even to this day I cannot go out to the bush without worrying that I might blunder into the clutches of a huge, red, drink-crazed kangaroo who may well be bearing a grudge against me.

# Pretty Sally
## C.J. Dennis

The diggers came from Bendigo,
From Albury the drovers,
From where the Goulburn waters flow
Came bearded teamsters travelling slow,
And all the brown bush rovers;
And where the road goes winding still
To drop to Melbourne valley,
They sought the shanty by the hill,
And called for beer and drank their fill,
And sparked with Pretty Sally.

The teamsters halted by the door
To give their horses water,
And stood about the bar-room floor
To ogle, while they had one more,
The shanty keeper's daughter.
Diggers with gold from creek and claim
About her used to rally,
Shearers and booted stockmen came
And to the hill they gave her name,
For all loved Pretty Sally.

I see her now; a sparkling lass
Brim-full of fun and laughter.
And where the slow teams used to pass,
And swagmen paused to beg a glass,
Now motor cars speed after.
And when I seek the road anew
That dips down to the valley,
I see again that bearded crew,
And, of the lovers, wonder who
At last wed Pretty Sally.

# The Story of "Gentleman-Once"
## Henry Lawson

Peter M'Laughlan, Bush missionary, Joe Wilson and his mate Jack Barnes, shearers for the present, and a casual swagman named Jack Mitchell were camped at Cox's Crossing in a bend of Eurunderee Creek.

It was a grassy little flat with gum trees standing clear and clean like a park. At the back was the steep grassy siding of a ridge, and far away across the creek to the south a spur from the Blue Mountain range ran west, with a tall, blue granite peak showing clear in the broad moonlight, yet dreamlike and distant over the sweeps of dark green bush.

There was the jingle of hobble-chain and a crunching at the grass where the horses moved in the soft shadows amongst the trees. Up the creek on the other side was a surveyors' camp, and from there now and again came the sound of a good voice singing verses of old songs; and later on the sound of a violin and a cornet being played, sometimes together and sometimes each on its own.

Wilson and Barnes were on their way home from shearing outback in the great scrubs of Beenaway Shed. They had been rescued by Peter M'Laughlan from a wayside shanty where they had fallen, in spite of mutual oaths and pat promises, sacred and profane, because they had got wringing wet in a storm on the track and caught colds, and had been tempted to take just one drink.

They were in a bad way, and were knocking down their cheques beautifully when Peter M'Laughlan came along. He rescued them and some of their cash from the soulless shanty keeper, and was riding home with them, on some pretence, because he had known them as boys, because Joe Wilson had a vein of poetry in him, because Jack Barnes had a dear little girl-wife who was much too good for him, and who was now anxiously waiting for him in the pretty little farming town of Solong amongst the western spurs. Because, perhaps, of something in Peter's early past which was a mystery. Simply and plainly because Peter M'Laughlan was the kindest, straightest and truest man in the West.

They all knew Mitchell and welcomed him heartily when he turned up in their camp, because he was a pathetic humorist and a kindly cynic — a "joker" or "hard-case" as the bushmen say.

Peter was about fifty and the other three were young men.

There was another man in camp who didn't count and was supposed to be dead. Old Danny Quinn, champion "beer-chewer" of the district, was on his way out, after a spree, to one of Rouse's stations, where, for the sake of past services — long past — and because of old times, he was supposed to be working. He had spent his last penny a week before, and had clung to his last-hope hotel until the landlord had taken him in one hand and his swag in the other and lifted them clear of the verandah. Danny had blundered on this far somehow. He was the last in the world who could have told how, and had managed to light a fire; then he lay with his head on his swag and enjoyed his own particularly lurid little hell undisturbed until Peter M'Laughlan and his mates came along. Peter gave him nips of whisky in judicious doses and at reasonable intervals, and later on a tot of mutton broth which he made in one of the billies.

It was after tea. Peter sat on a log by the fire with Joe and Jack Mitchell on one side and Jack Barnes on the other. Jack Mitchell sat on the grass with his back to the log, his knees drawn up, and his arms abroad on them: his most comfortable position and one which seemed to favour the flow of his philosophy. They talked of Bush things or reflected, sometimes all three together, sometimes by turns.

From the surveyors' camp:

*I remember, I remember,*
*The house where I was born,*
*The little window where the sun*
*Came peeping in at morn —*

The breeze from the west strengthened and the voice was blown away.

"That chap seems a bit sentimental but he's got a good voice," said Mitchell. Then presently he remarked, round his pipe, "I wonder if old Danny remembers?"

And presently Peter said quietly, as if the thought had just occurred to him, "By the way, Mitchell, I forgot to ask after your old folk. I knew your father, you know."

"Oh, they're all right, Peter, thank you."

"Heard from them lately?" asked Peter, presently, in a lazy tone.

Mitchell straightened himself up. "N-no. To tell the truth, Peter, I haven't written for … I don't know how long."

Peter smoked reflectively.

"I remember your father well, Jack," he said. "He was a big-hearted man."

Old Danny was heard remonstrating loudly with spirits from a warmer clime than Australia, and Peter stepped over to soothe him.

"I thought I'd get it, directly after I opened my mouth," said Mitchell. "I suppose it will be your turn next, Joe."

"I suppose so," said Joe, resignedly.

The wind fell.

*I remember, I remember,*
*And it gives me little joy,*
*To think I'm further off from heaven,*
*Than when I was a boy!*

When Peter came back another thought seemed to have occurred to him.

"How's your mother getting on, Joe?" he asked. "She shifted to Sydney after your father died, didn't she?"

"Oh, she's getting on all right!" said Joe, without elaboration.

"Keeping a boarding house, isn't she?"

"Yes," said Joe.

"Hard to make ends meet, I suppose?" said Peter. "It's almost a harder life than it could have been on the old selection, and there's none of the old independence about it. A woman like your mother must feel it, Joe."

"Oh, she's all right," said Joe. "She's used to it by this time. I manage to send her a few pounds now and again. I send her all I can," he added resentfully.

Peter sat corrected for a few moments. Then he seemed to change the subject.

"It's some time since you were in Sydney last, isn't it, Joe?"

"Yes, Peter," said Joe. "I haven't been there for two years. I never did any good there. I'm far better knocking about outback."

There was a pause.

"Some men seem to get on better in one place, some in another," reflected Mitchell lazily. "For my part, I seem to get on better in another."

Peter blinked, relit his pipe with a stick from the fire and reflected.

The surveyor's song had been encored:

*I remember, I remember …*

Perhaps Peter remembered. Joe did, but there were no vines round the house where he was born, only drought and dust, and raspy voices raised in recrimination, and hardship most times.

"I remember," said Peter, quietly, "I remember a young fellow at home in the old country. He had every advantage. He had a first-class education, a great deal more money than he needed, almost as much as he asked for, and nearly as much freedom as he wanted. His father was an English gentleman and his mother an English lady. They were titled people, if I remember rightly. The old man was proud but fond of his son; he only asked him to pay a little duty or respect now and again. We don't understand these things in Australia: they seem formal and cold to us. The son paid his respects to his father occasionally, a week or so before he'd be wanting money, as a rule. The mother was a dear lady. She idolised her son. She only asked for a little show of affection from him, a few days or a week of his society at home now and then, say once in three months. But he couldn't spare her even that, his time was taken up so much in fashionable London and Paris and other places. He would give the world to be able to take his proud, soft old father's hand now and look into his eyes as one man who understands another. He would be glad and eager to give his mother twelve months out of the year if he thought it would make her happier. It has been too late for more than twenty years."

Old Danny called for Peter.

Mitchell jerked his head approving and gave a sound like a sigh and chuckle conjoined, the one qualifying the other.

"I told you you'd get it, Joe," he said.

"I don't see how it hits me," said Joe.

"But it hit all the same, Joe."

"Well, I suppose it did," said Joe, after a short pause.

"He wouldn't have hit you so hard if you hadn't tried to parry," reflected Mitchell. "It's your turn now, Jack."

Jack Barnes said nothing.

"Now I know that Peter would do anything for a woman or

child, or an honest, straight, hard-up chap," said Mitchell, straightening out his legs and folding his arms, "but I can't quite understand his being so partial to drunken scamps and vagabonds, black sheep and ne'er-do-wells. He's got a tremendous sympathy for drunks. He'd do anything to help a drunken man. Ain't it marvellous? It's my private opinion that Peter must have been an awful boozer and scamp in his time."

The other two only thought. Mitchell was privileged. He was a young man of freckled, sandy complexion, and quizzical eyes. "Sly Joker"; "could take a rise out of anyone on the quiet"; "You could never tell when he was getting at you"; "face of a born comedian", as bushmen said of Mitchell. But he would probably have been a dead and dismal failure on any other stage than that of wide Australia.

Peter came back and they sat and smoked, and maybe they reflected along four very different back-tracks for a while.

The surveyor started to sing again:

*I have heard the mavis singing*
*Her love-song to the morn,*
*I have seen the dew-drop clinging*
*To the rose just newly born.*

They smoked and listened in silence all through to the end. It was very still. The full moon was high. The long white slender branches of a box tree stirred gently overhead; the she-oaks in the creek sighed as they are always sighing, and the southern peak seemed ever so far away.

*That has made me thine for ever!*
*Bonny Mary of Argyle.*

"Blarst my pipe!" exclaimed Mitchell, suddenly. "I beg your pardon, Peter. My pipe's always getting stuffed up," and he proceeded to shell out and clear his pipe.

The breeze had changed and strengthened. They heard the violin playing "Annie Laurie".

"They must be having a Scotch night in that camp to-night," said Mitchell. The voice came again:

*Maxwelton's braes are bonny,*
*Where early fa's the dew,*
*For 'twas there that Annie Laurie*
*Gie'd me her promise true …*

Mitchell threw out his arm impatiently.

"I wish they wouldn't play and sing those old songs," he said. "They make you think of damned old things. I beg your pardon, Peter."

Peter sat leaning forward, his elbows resting on his knees and his hands fingering his cold pipe nervously. His sad eyes had grown haggard and haunted. It is in the hearts of exiles in new lands that the old songs are felt.

"Take no thought of the morrow, Mitchell," said Peter, abstractedly. "I beg your pardon, Mitchell. I mean …"

"That's all right, Peter," said Mitchell. "You're right; tomorrow is the past, as far as I'm concerned."

Peter blinked down at him as if he were a new species.

"You're an odd young man, Mitchell," he said. "You'll have to take care of that head of yours or you'll be found hanging by a saddle strap to a leaning tree on a lonely track, or find yourself in a lunatic asylum before you're forty-five."

"Or else I'll be a great man," said Mitchell. "But — ah, well!"

Peter turned his eyes to the fire and smiled sadly.

"Not enjoyment and not sorrow, is our destined end or way," he repeated to the fire.

"But we get there just the same," said Mitchell, "destined or not."

*But to live, that each to-morrow,*
*Finds us further than today!*


"Why, that just my life, Peter," said Mitchell. "I might have to tramp two or three hundred miles before I get a cut in a shearing-shed or a job, and if tomorrow didn't find me nearer than today I'd starve or die of thirst on a dry stretch."

"Why don't you get married and settle down, Mitchell?" asked Peter, a little tired. "You're a teetotaller."

"If I got married I couldn't settle down," said Mitchell. "I reckon I'd be the loneliest man in Australia." Peter gave him a swift glance. "I reckon I'd be single no matter how much married I might be. I couldn't get the girl I wanted, and … ah, well!"

Mitchell's expression was still quaintly humorous round the lower part of his face, but there was a sad light in his eyes. The strange light as of the old dead days, and he was still young.

The cornet had started in the surveyors' camp.

"Their blooming tunes seem to fit in just as if they knew what we were talking about," remarked Mitchell.

The cornet:


*You'll break my heart, you little bird,*
*That sings upon the flowering thorn —*
*Thou minds't me or departed joys,*
*Departed never to return.*


"Damn it all," said Mitchell, sitting up, "I'm getting sentimental." Then, as if voicing something that was troubling him, "Don't you think a woman pulls a man down as often as she lifts him up, Peter?"

"Some say so," said Peter.

"Some say so, and they write it, too," said Mitchell.

"Sometimes it seems to me as if women were fated to drag a man down ever since Adam's time. If Adam hadn't taken his wife's advice — but there, perhaps he took her advice a good many times and found it good, and, just because she happened to be wrong this time, and to get him into a hole, the sons of Adam have never let the daughters of Eve hear the last of it. That's human nature."

Jack Barnes, the young husband, who was suffering a recovery, had been very silent all the evening. "I think a man's a fool to always listen to his wife's advice," he said, with the unreasonable impatience of a man who wants to think while others are talking. "She only messes him up, and drives him to the devil as likely as not, and gets a contempt for him in the end."

Peter gave him a surprised, reproachful look, and stood up. He paced backwards and forwards on the other side of the fire, with his hands behind his back for a while; then he came and settled himself on the log again and filled his pipe.

"Yes," he said, "a man can always find excuses for himself when his conscience stings him. He puts mud on the sting. Man at large is beginning all over the world to rake up excuses for himself; he disguises them as 'psychological studies', and thinks he is clean and clever and cultured, or he calls 'em problems — the sex problem, for instance, and thinks he is brave and fearless."

Danny was in trouble again, and Peter went to him. He complained that when he lay down he saw the faces worse, and he wanted to be propped up somehow, so Peter got a pack saddle and propped the old man's shoulders up with that.

"I remember," Peter began, when he came back to the fire, "I remember a young man who got married ..."

Mitchell hugged himself. He knew Jack Barnes. He knew that Jack had a girl-wife who was many times too good for him; that Jack had been wild, and had nearly broken her heart, and he had guessed at once that Jack had broken out again, and that Peter M'Laughlan was shepherding him home. Mitchell had worked as mates with Jack, and liked him because of the good heart that was in him in spite of all; and, because he liked him, he was glad that

Jack was going to get a kicking, so to speak, which might do him good. Mitchell saw it coming, as he said afterwards, and filled his pipe, and settled himself comfortably to listen.

"I remember the case of a naturally selfish young man who got married," said Peter. "He didn't know he was selfish; in fact, he thought he was too much the other way — but that doesn't matter now. His name was … well, we'll call him Gentleman-Once."

"Do you mean 'Gentleman-Once' that we saw drinking back at Thomas's shanty?" asked Joe.

"No," said Peter, "not him. There have been more than one in the Bush who went by the nickname of Gentleman Once. I knew one or two. It's a big clan, the clan of Gentleman Once, and scattered all over the world."

"By the way," said Mitchell — "excuse me for interrupting, Peter — but wasn't old Danny, there, a gentleman once? I've heard chaps say he way."

"I know he was," said Peter.

"Gentleman-Once! Who's talking about Gentleman-Once?" said an awful voice, suddenly and quickly. "About twenty or thirty years ago I was called Gentleman Once or Gentleman Jack. I don't know which, get out! *Get out*, I say! It's all lies, and you're the devil. There's four devils sitting by the fire. I see them."

Two of the four devils by the fire looked round, rather startled.

Danny was sitting up, his awful bloodshot eyes glaring in the firelight, and his ruined head looking like the bloated head of a hairy poodle that had been drowned and dried. Peter went to the old man and soothed him by waving off the snakes and devils with his hands, and telling them to go.

"I've heard Danny on the Gentleman-Once racket before," remarked Mitchell. "Seems funny, doesn't it, for a man to be proud of the fact that he was called Gentleman-Once about twenty years ago?"

"Seems more awful than funny to me," said Joe.

"You're right, Joe," said Mitchell. "But the saddest things are often funny."

When Peter came back he went on with his story, and was only interrupted once or twice by Danny waking up and calling him to drive off the snakes, and green and crimson dogs with crocodile heads, and devils with flaming tails, and those unpleasant sorts of things that force their company on boozers and madmen.

"Gentleman Once," said Peter, "he came from the old country with a good education and no character. He disgraced himself and family once too often and came, or was sent, out to Australia to reform. It's a great mistake. If a man is too far gone, or hasn't the strength to live the past down and reform at home, he won't do it in a new country, unless a combination of circumstances compel him to it. A man rises by chance; just as often he falls by chance. Some men fall into the habit of keeping steady and stick to it, for the novelty of it, until they are on their feet and in their sane minds and can look at the past, present and future sensibly. I knew one case … But that's got nothing to do with the story.

"Gentleman Once came out on the remittance system. That system is fatal in nine cases out of ten. The remittance system is an insult to any manhood that may be left in the black sheep, and an insult to the land he is sent to. The cursed quarterly allowance is a stone round his neck which will drag him down deeper in a new land than he would have fallen at home.

"You know that remittance men are regarded with such contempt in the Bush that a man seldom admits he is one, save when he's drunk and reckless and wants money or credit. When a ne'er-do-well lands in Melbourne or Sydney without a penny he will probably buck up and do something for himself. When he lands with money he will probably spend it all in the first few months and then straighten up, because he has to. But when he lands on the remittance system he drinks, first to drown homesickness. He decides that he'll wait till he gets his next quarter's allowance and then look round. He persuades himself that it's no use trying to do anything: that, in fact, he can't do anything until he gets his money. When he gets it he drifts into one "last" night with chums he has picked up in second- and third-rate hotels.

"He drinks from pure selfishness. No matter what precautions his friends at home take, he finds means of getting credit or drawing on his allowance before it is due — until he is two or three quarters behind. He drinks because he feels happy and jolly and clever and good-natured and brave and honest while he is drinking. Later on he drinks because he feels the reverse of all these things when he is sober. He drinks to drown the past and repentance. He doesn't know that a healthy-minded man doesn't waste time in repenting. He doesn't know how easy it is to reform, and is too weak-willed to try. He gets a muddled idea that the past can't be mended.

"He finds it easy to get drink and borrow money on the strength of his next quarter's allowance, so he soon gets a quarter or two behind, and sometimes gets into trouble connected with borrowed money. He drifts to the Bush and drinks, to drown the past only. The past grows blacker and blacker until it is a hell without repentance; and often the black sheep gets to that state when a man dreads his sober hours.

"And the end? Well, you see old Danny there, and you saw old 'Awful Example' back at Johnson's shanty, he's worse than Danny, if anything. Sometimes the end comes sooner. I saw a young new-land-new-leaf man dying in a cheap lodging house in Sydney. He was a school mate of mine, by the way. For six weeks he lay on his back and suffered as I never saw a man suffer in this world, and I've seen some bad cases. They had to chloroform him every time they wanted to move him. He had affected to be hard and cynical, and I must say that he played it out to the end. It was a strong character, a strong mind sodden and diseased with drink. He never spoke of home and his people except when he was delirious. He never spoke, even to me, of his mental agony. That was English home training. You young Australians wouldn't understand it; most bushmen are poets and emotional.

"My old school mate was shifted to the Sydney Hospital at last, and consented to the amputation of one leg. But it was too late. He was gone from the hips down. Drink, third-rate hotel and Bush shanty drink, and low debauchery."

Jack Barnes drew up his leg and rubbed it surreptitiously. He had "pins and needles". Mitchell noticed and turned a chuckle into a grunt.

"Gentleman Once was a remittance man," continued Peter. "But before he got very far he met an Australian girl in a boarding house. Her mother was the landlady. They were Bush people who had drifted to the city. The girl was pretty, intelligent and impulsive. She pitied him and nursed him. He wasn't known as Gentleman Once then, he hadn't got far enough to merit the nickname."

Peter paused. Presently he jerked his head as if he felt a spasm of pain, and leaned forward to get a stick from the fire to light his pipe.

"Now, there's the girl who marries a man to reform him, and when she has reformed him never lets him hear the last of it. Sometimes, as a woman, she drives him back again. But this was not one of that sort of girls. I once held a theory that sometimes a girl who has married a man and reformed him misses in the reformed man the something which attracted her in the careless scamp, the something which made her love him, and so she ceases to love him, and their married life is a far more miserable one than it would have been had he continued drinking. I hold no theory of that kind now. Such theories ruin many married lives."

Peter jerked his head again as if impatient with a thought, and reached for a firestick.

"But that's got nothing to do with the story. When Gentleman-Once reformed his natural selfishness came back. He saw that he had made a mistake. It's a terrible thing for a young man, a few months, perhaps a few weeks after his marriage, to ask himself the question, 'Have I made a mistake?' But Gentleman Once wasn't to be pitied. He discovered that he had married beneath him in intellect and education. Home training again. He couldn't have discovered that he had married beneath him as far as birth was concerned, for his wife's father had been a younger son of an older and greater family than his own. But Gentleman-Once wouldn't have been cad enough to bother about birth. I'll do him that much justice.

"He discovered, or thought he did, that he and his wife could never have one thought in common; that she couldn't possibly understand him. I'll tell you later on whether he was mistaken or not. He was gloomy most times, and she was a bright, sociable, busy little body. When she tried to draw him out of himself he grew irritable. Besides, having found that they couldn't have a thought in common he ceased to bother to talk to her. There are many men who don't bother talking to their wives; they don't think their wives feel it because the wives cease to complain after a while; they grow tired of trying to make the man realise how they suffer.

"Gentleman Once tried his best, according to his lights and weakness. Then he went in for self-pity and all the problems. He liked to brood, and his poor little wife's energy and cheerfulness were wearying to him. He wanted to be left alone. They were both high-spirited, in different ways; she was highly strung and so was he, because of his past life mostly. They quarrelled badly sometimes. Then he drank again and she stuck to him. Perhaps the only time he seemed cheerful and affectionate was when he had a few drinks in him. It was a miserable existence — a furnished room in a cheap lodging house, and the use of the kitchen.

"He drank alone.

"Now, a dipsomaniac mostly thinks he is in the right, except, perhaps, after he has been forced to be sober for a week. The noblest woman in the world couldn't save him. Everything she does to reform him irritates him; but a strong friend can save him sometimes, a man who has been through it himself. The poor little wife of Gentleman Once went through it all. And she stuck to him. She went into low pubs after him."

Peter shuddered again.

"She went through it all. He swore promises. He'd come home sober and fill her with hope of future happiness, and swear that he'd never take another glass. 'And we'll be happy yet, my poor boy,' she'd say, 'we'll be happy yet. I believe you, I trust you' (she used to call him her 'bonny boy' when they were first married). And next night he'd come home worse than ever. And one day he … he struck her!"

Peter shuddered, head and shoulders, like a man who had accidentally smashed his finger.

"And one day he struck her. He was sober when he did it, anyhow, he had not taken drink for a week. A man is never sober who gets drunk more than once a week, though he might think he is. I don't know how it happened, but anyway he struck her, and that frightened him. He got a billet in the Civil Service up country. No matter in what town it was. The little wife hoped for six months.

"I think it's a cruel thing that a carelessly selfish young man cannot realise how a sensitive young wife suffers for months after he has reformed. How she hopes and fears, how she dreads the moment he has to leave her, and frets every hour he is away from home, and suffers mental agony when he is late. How the horror of the wretched old past time grows upon her until she dares not think of it. How she listens to his step and voice and watches his face, when he comes home, for a sign of drink. A young man, a mate of mine, who drank hard and reformed, used to take a delight in pretending for a few minutes to be drunk when he came home. He was good-hearted, but dense. He said he only did it to give his wife a pleasant surprise afterwards. I thought it one of the most cruel things I had ever seen.

"Gentleman Once found that he could not stand the routine of office work and the dull life in that place. He commenced to drink again, and went on till he lost his billet. They had a little boy, a bright little boy, yet the father drank.

"The last spree was a terrible one. He was away from home a fortnight, and in that fortnight he got down as deep as a man could get. Then another man got hold of him and set him on his feet, and straightened him up. I don't hold that a man's salvation is always in his own hands; I've seen mates pull mates out of hell too often to think that.

"Then Gentleman Once saw the past as he had never seen it before, he saw hope for the future with it. And he swore an oath that he felt he would keep.

"He suffered from reaction on his way home, and, as he neared the town, a sudden fear, born of his nervous state, no doubt, sent a cold, sick emptiness through him; 'Was it too late?'

"As he turned into the street where he lived, he noticed a little group of Bush larrikins standing at the corner. And they moved uneasily when they caught sight of him, and, as he passed, they touched and lifted their hats to him. Now he knew that he had lost the respect even of Bush larrikins; and he knew enough of the Bush to know that a bushman never lifts his hat to a man, only a death, and a woman sometimes. He hurried home and read the truth in his wife's eyes. His little boy was dead. He went down under the blow, and she held his head to her breast and kept saying, 'My poor boy, my poor boy!'

"It was he that she meant, not the boy she had lost. She knew him, she understood him better than he did himself, and, heartbroken as she was, she knew how he was going to suffer, and comforted him. 'My poor boy, my poor, foolish boy!'

"He mended the past, as far as he could, during the next two years, and she seemed happy. He was very gentle, he was very kind to her. He was happy, too, in a new, strange way. But he learned what it was to suffer through his own fault, and now he was to learn what it was to suffer through no fault of his own, and without the consolation of saying 'I was wrong! I was to blame!' At the end of the two years there was another child, and his wife died."

The four sat silently smoking until Jack Barnes asked: "And what did he do then, Peter?"

"Who?" said Peter, abstractedly.

"Why, Gentleman Once."

Peter roused himself.

"Well, I've told the story, and it is about time to turn in," he said. "I can't say exactly what Gentleman Once did when his wife died. He might have gone down to a deeper depth than Danny's. He might have risen higher than he had ever been before. From what I knew of his character he would never have gone down an easy slope as Danny has done. He might have dropped plump at first and then climbed up. Anyway, he had the memory of the last two years to help him.

"Then there's the reformed drunkard who has trained himself to take a drink when he needs it, to drink in moderation, he's the strongest character of all, I think, but it's time to turn in."

The cornet up the creek was playing a march.

Peter walked across and looked at Danny, who seemed to be sleeping as peacefully as could be expected of him.

Jack Barnes got up and walked slowly down the creek in the moonlight. He wanted to think.

Peter rolled out his blankets on the grass and arranged his saddlebags for a pillow. Before he turned in Mitchell shook hands with him, a most unusual and unnecessary proceeding in camp. But there's something in the Bush grip which means, "I know", or, "I understand".

Joe Wilson rolled out his blankets close to Mitchell's camp; he wanted to enjoy some of Mitchell's quiet humour before he went to sleep, but Mitchell wasn't in a philosophical mood. He wanted to reflect.

"I wonder who Gentleman Once was?" said Joe to Mitchell. "Could he have been Danny, or old 'Awful Example' back there at the shanty?"

"Dunno," said Mitchell. He puffed three long puffs at his pipe, and then said, reflectively: "I've heard men tell their own stories before to-night, Joe."

It was Joe who wanted to think now.

About four o'clock Mitchell woke and stood up. Peter was lying rolled in his blanket with his face turned to the west. The moon was low, the shadows had shifted back, and the light was on Peter's face. Mitchell stood looking at him reverently, as a grown son might who see his father asleep for the first time. Then Mitchell quietly got some boughs and stuck them in the ground at a little distance from Peter's head, to shade his face from the bright moonlight; and then he turned in again to sleep till the sun woke him.

> "When houses seem devoid of heat,
> And hands are numb, howe'er one rubs,
> There yet remains one solace sweet,
> We go to drink in little pubs."
>
> HUGH MCCRAE, 1927

# The Day the Pub Didn't Burn Down
## Jim Haynes

It was the palm trees in the courtyard that caused all the trouble. The new publican at the Royal reckoned they were "a bit of an eyesore". They towered way above the galvanised iron roof and their thick grey trunks took up most of the room in the little courtyard bounded by the bar at the front, the washhouse and store along the sides and the guests' rooms along the back.

The ornamental berries and fronds used to shed regularly onto the pub roof and Old Jimmy the pub handyman reckoned he was, "Getting too old to be forever climbing up on the bloody roof."

Win Jenkins, who did the cleaning and laundry at the Royal, agreed with him. She was sick of the mess around the courtyard floor causing her a lot of extra work and she voiced this opinion to anyone who would listen. Indeed she spent a lot more time voicing this opinion than she did actually cleaning up the mess in the courtyard.

There wasn't that much cleaning done at the Royal, to be honest. Being the town's "other pub" meant that a high standard of cleanliness was not really expected. There wasn't much laundry because people only stayed there by mistake, and usually only once. Mopping out the front bar and hosing down the verandah were the main cleaning tasks, and when the pub lived up to its reputation of being "the bloodhouse" this changed to hosing out the front bar as well, rather than persevering with a mop.

Nevertheless, Win was of the opinion that "those bloody old palm trees" made her life a lot harder, and she joined with Jimmy in telling the new publican that the pub would be better off without them. The new publican listened and nodded.

The trees might still have been safe if these had been the only voices speaking out against them. After all Jimmy and Win had said the same thing to a succession of new publicans. But a couple of other factors also conspired against them. The first of these was that Dot, the barmaid at the Royal, had also decided the trees were a "bloody nuisance".

This was a new development. As a rule Dot didn't bother herself with the territory beyond the bar at the Royal, she didn't need to. Dot ruled the Royal with a fist of iron from the front bar. She didn't need to visit the courtyard or the laundry as long as she controlled the front bar of the Royal.

Dot was a legend in Weelabarabak. Her standard greeting, "Waddya want?", actually set the standard for small town hospitality for miles around. She could prevent a brawl with one word from twenty paces and she possessed an icy stare that could make a drunken shearer think twice about causing trouble.

Nobody really knew why Dot suddenly took an interest in the palm trees. I reckon she just got sick of Win and Jimmy whingeing and decided to resolve the matter by agreeing with them. Whatever the reason, she added her considerable weight to the decision by telling the new publican he should "get rid of the bloody things".

This onslaught on the new publican occurred very soon after his arrival at the Royal. The staff knew you didn't have much time to initiate change before a new publican sank into the same state of apathy as all his predecessors and did pretty much nothing except let Dot run the pub from the front bar. So the plot against the palm trees was hatched during his first week in the place.

Even then, it might not have succeeded except for one other factor. The new publican had just come from managing a series of pubs that had all been destroyed by fire. He was not quite stupid enough to believe that these fires had been complete accidents as on at least one occasion he had been told to be away from the premises at a specified time. He was also well aware that the actual owners of these establishments had benefited rather nicely from the demise of each pub.

These experiences had left him wary of sudden fires in the night. He hadn't *always* been told to be away from the premises on relevant dates it seems, and he had consequently become a bit jumpy about the prospect of sudden fires.

So the new publican, in light of the staff conspiracy against the palm trees — or perhaps solely for reasons of his own — decided the palm trees were a fire hazard and he decided to solve this problem in a unique way. He decided to burn them down.

Well, they were too tall to cut down; they would have caused quite a lot of damage when they fell onto the roof. And that's where they would have fallen because the courtyard was so small. They would have fallen on the bar, the store, the laundry or the guests' rooms, causing who knew how much damage. The new publican no doubt thought the palm trees would burn in a quite orderly manner, disintegrating into a fairly neat pile of coal and ash within the courtyard.

He set fire to them quite early one morning, expecting the whole thing to be over and cleaned up by lunchtime. He soaked the trunks with kero and piled some kindling and stove wood around each base and up the fire went, racing on kero fumes into the foliage at the top of each tree. An excited mob of kids and grownups assembled from nowhere to enjoy that strange communal thrill humans always seem to experience in the presence of a really destructive fire. We were on our way to school as the fire took off, and quickly diverted our course down the side street next to the pub to watch the proceedings, wheeling our bikes as close as we dared so we could see the whole scene inside the courtyard.

The fronds and greenery at the top of the trees burned away very quickly. In a quite spectacular display the burning vegetation fell to earth in and around the courtyard and on the galvanised iron roof where it quickly burnt out, leaving a mess of ash to be cleaned up later on by Win and Jimmy. We "oohed" and "arrghed" in time to the bursts of flame and the falling of the largest pieces of burning vegetation and tried to ignore the adults who told us to "look out" and "get off to bloody school and out of the way".

After that the fire settled down and became rather boring. The thick spongy trunks burned away slowly, apparently from the inside. As they smouldered the trunks turned blacker and blacker and a steady column of grey smoke arose from each one and drifted lazily into the clear sky above the courtyard of the Royal Hotel.

After the early spectacle of the blazing vegetation and fiery falling fronds this was rather mundane to watch and soon the group of onlookers had completely disintegrated, we reluctantly headed to school and the town went about its business.

By lunchtime the new publican had discovered that burning palm trees smoulder for an amazingly long time. So long did they smoulder in fact that they had practically been forgotten when the wind strengthened out of the west at about three o'clock that afternoon, just about the same time that the trees really began to disintegrate and fall apart. They had now become two teetering columns of glowing coals and, as the wind picked up, they began raining red hot embers and quite sizeable lumps of fire all over the pub and its surroundings.

As the hot wind gusted out of a still clear sky the scene began to resemble something out of a medieval painting of Judgment Day or one of those particularly lurid Old Testament illustrations we were shown in Sunday school — the ones where Egypt suffered plagues and torments because Pharaoh wouldn't let the Israelites go.

These falling embers were far more substantial than the morning shower of burning fronds. The coals continued to burn with substantial intensity upon hitting the ground, the roof, the dry grass around the pub, or the wooden verandahs and walkways inside the courtyard and along the main street in front of the pub.

In fact by three-twenty, when Mrs Thompson was telling us to tidy up our desks and make sure we'd written our homework into our homework books, the Royal Hotel was in mortal danger of transforming itself from the town's "other pub" into the town's "ex-pub". The new publican and the few staff who were on duty, along with the few desperate afternoon drinkers, had been galvanised into action, some were filling buckets from the cement tubs in the wash house and others had been despatched to get help from nearby businesses and dwellings while warning them of the possible danger.

In the midst of the growing hysteria Dot the barmaid arrived to start her normal shift. She took one look at the scene, lifted the phone and told the postmaster to call out the Weelabarabak fire brigade.

Luckily this was back in the days when the postmaster kept a key to the fire shed, whether he was fire captain or not. So the postmaster closed the post office and, along with his postal clerk and a couple of farmers who happened to be collecting mail at the time, raced to the nearby fire shed, opened the door and were all magically transformed into the Weelabarabak fire brigade.

The Weelabarabak fire shed contained the fire trailer which held the brigade's water tank, pump and hose. The Weelabarabak fire brigade did not possess a vehicle; the trailer had to be attached to the towbar of the nearest vehicle which possessed a towbar and could be commandeered in order to get the fire-fighting equipment to the actual fire.

As the small group of firemen entered the shed, however, the postal clerk, the brightest of the group, made the observation that the Royal was actually *downhill* from the fire shed and, if they filled the water tank *after* they arrived at the scene of the alleged fire rather than before they left the fire shed, the trailer would be light enough for them to push it to the Royal rather than waste time looking for a vehicle with a towbar. They could then fill the tank from the water mains at the pub and use the pump to direct the water with the necessary force onto the fire.

Gil Stafford had closed his produce store and dashed across the road to become part of the Weelabarabak fire brigade while the original group was opening the fire shed. It was Gil who made the suggestion at this point that perhaps the water mains could be connected directly to the brigade pump, thus making the water tank redundant. Encouraged by the general response that "it sounds like a good idea", Gil grabbed the length of hose designed to siphon water from rivers and dams into the pump and dashed back to his store to see if he had suitable fittings for its other end.

Meanwhile, the remainder of the Weelabarabak Fire Brigade (a remainder which was growing larger by the minute as local businesses closed and able-bodied men arrived) wheeled the trailer out of the fire shed and began pushing it in the direction of the endangered Royal Hotel. They left the water tank on board for two reasons, "just in case" and "take too long to get off", and those who couldn't find a space to help push gathered up sundry items from the fire shed, shovels, buckets etc., and ran behind, beside, or in front of the trailer.

The arrival of this enthusiastic caravan outside the Royal Hotel coincided with our arrival from school, which happened to be in the opposite direction. The coming together of these two groups, one made up of kids yelling rather obvious news of fires and fire brigades to each another and the other consisting of a trailer, on which everything rattled, bouncing along at terrifying speed accompanied by a dozen or so men thumping along in work boots and yelling at us to "look out", is certainly the noisiest memory I have of my childhood. But the visual memories I have of that scene, and what happened next, are even better.

In the midst of the confusion Gil Stafford had arrived with an armful of fittings and located the water main under the pub verandah. Stilsons were applied to the appropriate connections and, with a minimum of fuss and water wastage, the mains were connected to the pump. Now the pressure should have been sufficient to blast the necessary stream of water at the bits of the pub that had started to burn rather seriously and, of course, the remains of the trees themselves, now glowing chimneys of chaos and destruction.

The pump was started after a few good pulls on the rotor and it sprang into deafening life with a roar and a billow of smoke much blacker than that now arising from various parts of the pub. The short hose from the mains was connected to the intake at the back of the pump and now the fire hose was rolled out and connected to the front of the pump. It unwound up the steps, across the verandah, in the front door of the bar and out through the back door into the courtyard like a vengeful canvas python.

The men of the Weelabarabak fire brigade positioned themselves at intervals of a yard or so along the length of the fire hose. They were ready to take the strain like a tug-o'-war team, ready to control the deadly force of water about to be unleashed against the flames which threatened the Royal Hotel.

Us kids were told to "stand well back" and the word was given to turn the valve and let the pump do its work.

Nobody could remember when the hose had last been checked. It was a rule of the Weelabarabak fire brigade that the hose be checked annually "in case of *no fire*". In other words if the hose was not used for twelve months and there were no fires, it should be checked to see that it was still in an operational condition. The problem was that blokes got busy through the year and fire drill wasn't always as regular as it should be. Besides, no one really made a note of whether or not the hose was used when the brigade was called out and there wasn't always time for a working bee between fires, even if the time between fires stretched into years.

Evidently the hose, made of some kind of rubberised compound covered in canvas, had not been checked for quite a while. The resulting attempt at fire-fighting was spectacular. I can still see it now after all these years.

The water hit the first kink in the hose, where it turned an angle of twenty degrees or so from the trailer to the pub steps and a jet shot out of the hose, soaked the postmaster and arced some fifteen feet into the air. A yard further down the hose another stream of water shot out all over the postal clerk, then another stream broke out just under the verandah roof. It went straight up, hit the galvanised iron and cascaded down over all those on the verandah.

Just at the door of the pub a double stream shot out laterally hitting both sides of the door frame. Inside the bar jets continued to spout, at the floor, the wall and the ceiling. Each new spout was just as unexpected as the first and left men jumping and swearing along the length of the hose. It was as if the flow of water was accompanied by some weird electric current.

What we couldn't see from our position outside the pub was that each new eruption of water from the hose was measurably weaker than the last. The funniest scene of all, according to Old Nugget who was inside and told Dad and me later, through tears of laughter involved the two burliest farmers who stood braced in the door from the bar to the courtyard with the hose nozzle directed at the worst of the fire.

As the jets of water breaking from the hose became weaker and weaker, they stood steadfast and resolute, waiting to give the force of water its final direction. But when the stream did reach them it was not a fearsome pub-saving gusher of white water into the depths of the ravening fire. It was, in Nugget's own words, "a woeful little piddle of water which dribbled out the nozzle of the hose and splashed around their boots".

While chaos ruled in the bar and on the verandah and a forlorn puddle formed at the fire-fighting farmers' feet, the fire raged on in the courtyard, totally unaffected by the large amount of misdirected human energy being expended in futile attempts to extinguish it.

Theories and remedies for the situation abounded among the men of the Weelabarabak fire brigade, most of whom were soaked to the skin, but before they formulated a really useful Plan B, Dot had organised a bucket brigade from the wash house.

The fires in the courtyard, in the grass around the pub and in various other places, were quickly put out. The soaked firefighters joined in meekly, doing exactly as Dot told them until all was under control.

The palm trees were replaced on one side of the courtyard by a half-hearted barbecue and on the other by a new rotary clothesline. This was meant to make Win's life a bit easier, although she whinged a fair bit that it wouldn't keep still when you were pegging stuff on it. And they reckon that's the cleanest the bar of the Royal has ever been, before or since.

# Xmas Food Annoys Us
## Lennie Lower

Every time we hear a rooster crow, we feel sick. Ever since Xmas Day.

We know you don't want to hear anything about Xmas Day, but some well-meaning friends have invited us to a New Year's Eve dinner. It threatens to be something like Xmas dinner, and we're not going.

It's about time somebody with a certain amount of influence, like us, said something about this dinner business.

We've gone to an enormous lot of trouble to get Monsieur Patrick O'Reilly, head chef at the Hole in the Wall, to compile an ideal menu for *next* year.

"Ze — what you say? — ze cocktail, 'e should come first. For zis eet is best one pint of cold beer. Eef eet is to be a beeg dinner, three pints of cold beer," said M. O'Reilly.

The chef's suggested menu is:-

PRAWNS AVEC WHISKERS
Soup (off)
'Arf and 'arf


BEER
Curried Tongue avec spuds

BEER
Set of Smalls avec floor varnish or sauce;
Single aux peas

MORE BEER
Prawns avec whiskers

ALE

"Ze menu is veree sniftaire and bonzaire," said the chef. "Eet is so much bettaire to eat 'im standing up. One can zen chase ze little pea when 'e pop off ze knife, wizout knocking ze chair ovair."

A very sensible idea, too.

> "There is nothing which has yet been contrived by man, by which so much happiness is produced as by a good tavern or inn."
>
> Dr Samuel Johnson, 1776

# The Pub that Lost its Licence
## Henry Lawson

The pub that lost its licence
Was very quaint and old;
'Twas built before the railway,
Before the days of gold.
The pub that lost its licence
Was built of solid stone
And good Australian hardwood
In fashion all its own.

They build of bricks and softwood
Their narrow shells and high;
They build with iron girders
And build 'em to the sky:
The "joiners" rush and hurry,
Time-hunted men they are —
And "decorators" chase them
To "fit" the shoddy bar.

The little inn with gables
Rose slowly in the past,
In days when ships and houses
And men were built to last;
In dove-tailed days, and polished,

When "slumming" was a sin:
They fashioned it for comfort,
And called it "Fig Tree Inn".

Deep windowed and deep seated,
And fireplaces deep,
With a stone wall round the garden,
Where the vines of ages creep;
And sunny nooks and corners,
Where one might doze and sleep.
And seats on broad verandahs,
And a bar-room cool and deep.

Our public bars are seatless
In days of greed and rush —
Where fat casks stood, and tables,
Now men must stand and "lush".
The pub that lost its licence
Gave time to talk and think,
But nowadays old cronies
Must elbow up and drink.

Still round the ancient fig tree
The rustic table stands,
Surrounded by its benching
As 'twas in other lands;
Beneath it smiles the harbour,
The shippin' and all that;
And there, on summer Sundays,
Our fathers' fathers sat.

The publicans were stout men,
With manners wise and slow,
And so I sat with cronies

Not very long ago.
The stout and bustling landlady
While slowly ran the sands
Of life, where armchaired "granny"
Would doze with folded hands.

The furniture was ancient,
And heavy as 'twas strong,
Above hung watercolours
Of scenes, ah! vanished long,
Of blacks, and teams, and windmills,
Of homes beyond the seas:
And stern, unyielding pictures
Of old celebrities.

And boomerangs and waddies,
And sharks' teeth and whales' corns,
And, velveted and polished,
Some mighty bullock horns.
And spears in thongs of greenhide,
And tomahawks of stone,
And ancient guns and pistols,
And other things unknown.

The old pub lost its licence,
Not for its sins at all.
But because it was a free house!
(They said it was too small)
'Twas let to other people
That grind and grub, and wowse —
They turned it into "lodgings"
And called it "Fig Tree House".
(They opened it for boarders
And called it "Fig Tree House"!)

But 'twas haunted by the spirits
Of a better braver day,
They could not let the lodgings,
The boarders would not stay.
And so it stands deserted,
While, through new paint cheap and thin,
You might discern by moonlight
The old sign, "Fig Tree Inn".